AF660049

Letting Go

LETTING GO
A Novel

AMRINDER BAJAJ

BLOOMSBURY
NEW DELHI • LONDON • OXFORD • NEW YORK • SYDNEY

BLOOMSBURY INDIA
Bloomsbury Publishing India Pvt. Ltd
Second Floor, LSC Building No. 4, DDA Complex, Pocket C – 6 & 7,
Vasant Kunj, New Delhi, 110070

BLOOMSBURY, BLOOMSBURY INDIA and the Diana logo
are trademarks of Bloomsbury Publishing Plc

First published in India 2024
This edition published 2024

Copyright © Amrinder Bajaj, 2024

Amrinder Bajaj has asserted her right under the Indian Copyright Act
to be identified as the Author of this work

This is a work of fiction. Unless otherwise indicated, all the names, characters, businesses, places, events and incidents in this book are either the product of the author's imagination or used in a fictitious manner. Any resemblance to actual persons, living or dead, or actual events is purely coincidental

All rights reserved. No part of this publication may be reproduced or transmitted in any form or by any means, electronic or mechanical, including photocopying, recording or any information storage or retrieval system, without the prior permission in writing from the publishers

This book is solely the responsibility of the author and the publisher has had no role in the creation of the content and does not have responsibility for anything defamatory or libellous or objectionable

ISBN: PB: 978-93-56401-21-1; eBook: 978-93-56401-23-5
2 4 6 8 10 9 7 5 3 1

Typeset in Minion Pro by Manipal Technologies Limited
Printed and bound in India by Thomson Press India Ltd

MIX
Paper | Supporting responsible forestry
FSC® C010615
FSC www.fsc.org

To find out more about our authors and books visit www.bloomsbury.com and sign up for our newsletters

For
Khushwant Singh
my reluctant mentor

‘Dying even more than death defines the illness.’

The Emperor of All Maladies, Siddhartha Mukherjee

PART 1

2013

The unflushed toilet was where it all began. My husband would not lift the seat before peeing, and in my hurry to evacuate a menopausal bladder, I would end up sitting on the golden drops he left behind. You can only imagine the kind of retaliation this provoked! As if this was not bad enough, he never flushed after peeing. His lack of toilet etiquette was just one of his atrocious habits.

The other was his pathological stinginess, which affected almost every aspect of our married life. He took a sadistic pleasure in robbing me of my sleep in the hot Delhi summer. Complaints such as 'My husband does not let me sleep a wink at night' or 'My husband does not allow me a moment's peace at night' triggered envious glances from friends and an arch 'Is he that sexy?'

'Hell, no! He switches off the AC and I wake up in the middle of the night drenched in sweat!'

The financial dynamics of our household were strange. Our income was never clubbed, but our expenditures were divided, and he paid the electricity bill. So almost every night, I would wake up hot and flustered. With mounting anger and deep resentment, I would switch on the AC again. If I did not get proper sleep, how was I, an obstetrician and gynaecologist, to perform early morning surgeries or get rest after midnight deliveries? He tortured me in this way so that I would take on this expense too. I had fallen into his trap regarding the sly transfer of expenditure onto me but had cottoned on to his tactics and was determined not to give in any more. If I had to spend on everything, what did I need a husband for?

As if robbing me of my night's sleep was not torture enough, MS would wake me up early on the flimsiest of pretexts, knowing full well that I was not a morning person.

As a result, I would get up with a throbbing headache and a foul mood. And it fell on my hapless staff to bear the brunt of his horrible behaviour. Even the 30-minute power naps I took in the afternoons were unacceptable and he had to disturb me with questions like '*So gayi kya* (Are you sleeping)?' knowing full well that once awakened I could not fall asleep again. Little things like these gave birth to big hurts, for they showed how unimportant I was to him.

A wet towel, a comb full of hair, the uncapped Fixo bottle (the sticky washable glue with which Sikhs groom their uncut beard and paste it in place) on the bed, dirty clothes scattered on the floor, all were clues of my husband's activities from the time he got up to the time he left for his clinic. Then there were his killer smells that needed Herculean endurance. I wish the deadly combination of halitosis and body odour were grounds enough for divorce. Also to be endured was the smell of sweat-soaked clothes that he hung on pegs behind the bathroom door – putting them in the laundry basket was beneath him. I would almost pass out while reaching up to latch the bathroom door!

Weren't these habits bad enough to drive a woman away? But no, because he did not smoke, drink or womanise, he was a wonderful man and I ought to be grateful to be his wife, said my dear family. They could never understand why I was in a perpetual state of irritation with such a husband. They did not have to endure his stinginess – down to skimping on onions, which I liked in my salad, because they cost too much – the early morning darshan of an unflushed toilet and his odours about which he did nothing despite being a doctor.

Surprisingly, we had effectively overcome major acts of commission that could have broken any other marriage. That he had once gambled away our entire life's earnings (mine, after making a duplicate key of my almirah) and the large sums he had borrowed, leaving us penniless and in debt, could have ended our marriage but it did not. Instead, I pawned my jewellery to help him repay the loans he had taken to indulge in his addiction. Disillusionment led me to seek solace in another man's arms. Surprisingly, this too did not lead to divorce, for MS would not set me free though I wanted to marry Rajan. Perhaps the stigma of not being man enough for his wife was too much to bear; perhaps he took a perverse pleasure in keeping me against my will. Perhaps my income made him overlook my trespasses. It certainly was not out of love. I stayed back because of my sons, Karan and Simar, though they did not escape unscathed and would occasionally vent by lashing out at me. Now they were too engrossed in their own lives – one in another city, the other in another country – to bother about us. That Rajan, for whom I had risked everything, did not turn out to be worthy of my affections contributed considerably to the morbidity of my existence. Though we are no longer lovers, we are still in touch, chiefly over the phone. Being a go-getter, he continued to help me with many a civic and legal issue as MS was of no use in such matters.

With my wings effectively clipped, flutterings for freedom have long ceased. Over the years, I became resigned to my gilded cage. Acute antipathies have been reduced to chronic irritants that I have learnt to live with. After years of acrimonious matrimony, MS and I have settled into amiable incompatibility. Neither of us mentioned his love for the dice or mine for another man ever again. Despite the turbulent waters that have flowed under (sometimes over) the bridge, living with a person for nearly forty years has become a habit, and habits are stronger than love. There is no sharing of confidences, no cuddling up to each other in bed, but that never was in our marriage. We talk of mundane matters like a leaking faucet, a wedding in the extended family, and we still have our spats – chiefly over money. I argue just to make a point, for I understand that his stinginess is a personality flaw that cannot be rectified.

Living exclusively with the man I resented all my life did not prove as difficult as I had anticipated. Despite our differences, I have much to be grateful for. Meals are not eaten alone, I have an escort for social events and I do not have to sleep in an empty house at night. I have zero expectations from him, which has heralded the end of all quarrels. Mostly, he does his thing and I do mine without impinging upon each other's space. In fact, space is all that we give each other these days. The solitude that such a marriage provides is conducive to the pursuit of my passion for the written word and I take full advantage of it. All said and done, I am not unhappy. My cup of joy brimmed over when we recently became proud grandparents of a beautiful baby boy.

I never thought that a day would come when I would thank God for my husband's appalling civic sense. It was due to his abominable habit of not pulling the flush that I realised that the yellow in the pot had turned pink. When I mentioned it to MS, he brushed it off as a matter of no consequence.

'There is blood in your urine! This is not something that you can neglect,' I said.

'Must be because of the beetroot in the salad.'

'What nonsense! All of us ate it and none of us have discoloured urine. At the most, it stains the stools at times.' But I thereafter connected beetroot with cancer and could never bring myself to eat it again.

MS was terribly hassled about the shop in which he ran his clinic. The fate of his long-established medical practice hung in the balance and the stress was unbearable. The multistoreyed building that housed his clinic had been sold and the five people, including MS, who earned their livelihood from the shops located on the ground floor were told to vacate it. Besides MS, there was a photographer, a jeweller, a tailor and a general store merchant. They had paid a huge pagri, that is, a large lump sum, to the owner, which meant they paid a nominal monthly rent. As a result, they practically owned the place, but the new owner did not think so. All five had come here as bachelors, had married, reared children and got their children married with the income earned from these very premises. Now when they had all aged, the very source of their income was being snatched. Desperately, they were negotiating with the new owners for the purchase of their individual shops at subsidised rates. The new owners knew that it was not easy to evict such old tenants, but if a court battle ensued it could take years to reach a settlement. Numerous meetings were held but nothing concrete had come out as yet. If the deal fell through all would be lost. It was too expensive to buy another place, and building a new practice elsewhere this late in the day was no easy task. All this was taking a toll on MS's mental health, for his practice was his life.

I shared a love–hate relationship with the clinic and would often call it 'meri saut' (the other woman). It ate up chunks of family life, kept me waiting for hours, hungry and sleepy, till MS deemed it fit to leave her and have dinner with me. We were the last to reach any social function or wedding and had to eat leftovers after most of the guests had left. We never went on holidays (except for a few days to his parents' place), for he could not be parted from his clinic. Though I never got to see the fruit of such earnest endeavour, there was no arguing the fact that his clinic was dearer to him than his wife. When I was in labour with our first child, there was no anxious husband hovering around. He ditched me for his clinic at the most momentous moment of our lives. To my horror, he was not available to give his signature for an emergency caesarean section! The baby's heart rate had dropped and brain damage could ensue due to oxygen deprivation. Though I urged my obstetrician to perform the surgery without him, it was a medicolegal mandate that could not be bypassed. The agonies I suffered during the hour it took MS to reach the hospital from his precious clinic! Every extra excruciating labour pain counted; every minute a distressed baby struggled to get out of the suffocating environment of the womb counted. The very well-being of our unborn child was being jeopardised by his callous father! God, how I hated him and his clinic then.

But a day would come when I would be thankful for his obsession with it. So strong was his desire to go back to work that it became his sole incentive to live.

As of now, the latest on the clinic front was that the new owner intended to raze the building and build a swanky new structure in its place. MS was distraught and I had to bear the brunt of his dark moods. Not even his health issues could take his attention away from his professional future, or the lack of it. Just when he thought all was lost, a glimmer of hope appeared on the horizon. The new owner finally decided to let the tenants buy their shops at concessional rates. Leaving the shops untouched, he would build a new floor on their roofs so that their business would not be obstructed in any way. This was very good news indeed. Meanwhile, the colour of his urine had deepened from pale pink to pinkish-red, but he paid no heed to my entreaties to see a urologist for his painless haematuria.

'It could be anything – a polyp or a stone,' I said, knowing some stones are painless, but he couldn't care less. Never in my wildest dreams did I think that it could be cancer. People have died due to heart attacks, stroke and airway disease in our families, but so far cancer had never impinged on our lives. It did not occur to either of us that it would creep stealthily in, destroying all in its wake.

'Now that the matter of your clinic has been settled, get yourself investigated,' I pleaded, but there was still the unfinished business of arranging the finances. He wanted to get the shop registered in his name before the new owner changed his mind. As there was no pain, he told me categorically not to nag him. 'Do what you like,' I said in exasperation and left it at that. We had recently been blessed with a grandson and I decided to savour my newfound happiness. I focused my attention on the joyful activities that followed his birth.

After eight years of marriage, three years of intensive investigations for infertility, one failed IVF cycle, at immense emotional and monetary expense, my daughter-in-law Mona finally conceived. Happily, I had shelled out the money required for the second IVF and had driven halfway across Delhi to be with her for every procedure at the fertility centre and was overjoyed to learn that this time the beta HCG was positive. Our happiness was laced with apprehension, for there was a period of nine months to traverse between conception and birth. Mona had spotting issues in early pregnancy and a fainting attack which kept me on tenterhooks both as a would-be grandma and as her obstetrician.

Now that they had shifted to Delhi, I expected Simar and Mona to stay with me during this delicate period but they chose to live separately; so be it. All was forgiven at the birth of a baby boy. I was delirious with joy and distributed gifts in cash and kind including gold ornaments to all and sundry, besides fulfilling the umpteen mannats I had made. Why, the hijras alone took seventy-five rupees plus a sari and a gold nose-pin! Out of gratitude, I gave Mona an emerald, sapphire and ruby set complete with a necklace, earrings and a bracelet! Money flowed like water (my money, for MS was saving to buy the clinic) and a happy fatigue overwhelmed me. The hustle and bustle and the expenditure were almost like those of a wedding. Relatives came from all over India for the naming ceremony. It was during this time that others too noted the red colour in the toilet that remained unflushed and scolded him roundly for not doing anything about it.

How the gods must be laughing at the naivety of humans. In the first week of January, after Jessy, my grandson, was born, I was the happiest person on earth. In the first week of February, I thought I was the unhappiest person on this earth because Mona snatched Jessy from my arms to take him to her parents' place. Simar just stood by watching my misery, just as his father had done years ago when *his* mother had snatched *my* baby Karan from my arms to give him to her childless elder son! Tears had coursed down my cheeks then as they did now. I averted my face lest I be ridiculed for my public display of sorrow. It was not as if I did not want Mona's parents to savour the presence of the newborn, for he was their grandchild too, but Simar had got a job in Bengaluru and Mona's parents would anyway be going along with them in a month's time to mind the baby. They could enjoy him then to their heart's content. What was the need to deprive me now when Jessy was here for just a month more? Was it too much to ask for a few more days with my grandson during the short time they were in Delhi? This sorrow was but a foretaste of what was to come.

Now that we were no longer restricted by the presence of my son's new family, we were free to attend a medical conference in Amritsar. We enjoyed the journey, the company and the event. It was exactly what the doctor had prescribed to de-stress. The academic session lasted for only half a day at the five-star hotel where we were putting up. After lunch we were free to go shopping, visit the Golden Temple, explore the various landmarks, like Jallianwala Bagh, and enjoy the cuisine of this historic city. We went to the Wagah border, watched the ceremonial lowering of flags, which gave me goosebumps, and, despite the drizzle, danced with patriotic fervour. At night there was dance, karaoke and much revelry. We bought phulkari dupattas and the famed Amritsari papad and vadia to spice up our meals. It was a thoroughly enjoyable trip except for MS's terrible toilet habits. The one major change was that the drops he now left on the toilet rim were red instead of yellow. In a hurry to evacuate a bursting bladder, I saw them only when it was too late and plonked on the seat and stained my brand-new silk salwar. I charged like a raging bull at him with the choicest expletives.

'I am going to the dining hall,' was all he said.

By the time I changed and joined him, the fire of my fury had been doused by the icy fingers of fear. Such frank haematuria was ominous and I was seriously alarmed. We had to find the cause. Once back in Delhi, I insisted that he do something about it and soon. He got his urine tested and thought that the infection that showed up was the cause of his haematuria. When a course of antibiotics made no difference, I asked him to get an ultrasound done but so obsessed was he with the fate of his clinic that he disregarded the fate of his life. It was as if he was doing me a favour by taking care of his own health. Perhaps he was, for eventually I bore the brunt of his illness. Finally, a deal was struck and the five long-time occupants could buy a shop each for twenty-eight lakh rupees though the market rate was sixty lakh rupees. MS was jubilant, little knowing that he had won but a skirmish against fate and the battle for his very life was about to begin. On 27 February 2013, a Wednesday, he finally got the shop registered in his name.

The very next day I sent him to the ultrasound clinic. The scans showed a 3 cm x 2 cm growth in his bladder and another 0.9 cm growth beneath it. I called him but he did not answer the phone. Lunchtime came and went without MS or a word from him. In desperation I rang up Dr Pankaj, the owner of the diagnostic centre, and learnt that, fearing the worst, he had insisted that MS get a CECT done immediately. Phones were not allowed inside, but the least the heartless man could have done was inform me before going in for the procedure. I would have been spared fears about road accidents, broken bones and a dead body in the mortuary.

A while later I rang up the radiologist to enquire about the CECT results and learnt that he suspected the worst. My mouth went dry and my body got cold all over. Such was the urgency of the situation that he suggested that we get an MRI done that very night. Thus it came about that two distressed souls met for a date at an eerily empty diagnostic centre at 10 p.m. MS reached directly from his clinic while I came from home. An MRI is definitely not for the claustrophobic. The clanking of magnets deep in its recesses sounded like the chains that bound slaves to the dark belly of ancient ships. Dim lights cast eerie shadows on the walls. It was past midnight when the MRI was over.

Going beyond the limits of civility, Dr Pankaj got all the preoperative investigations done, for it was a given that the mass would need immediate intervention. He charged us not a penny for his urgent, extensive services and I blessed him from the bottom of my heart.

1.3.13

The MRI reports have just been delivered at home and MS is still at his clinic. I am all alone but cannot bring myself to open them. I postpone viewing the verdict till I finish the last unnecessary chore I foisted upon myself. Finally, with no excuse left, I take out the sheaf of films from the envelope with trembling hands. My heart sinks and my eyes blur when I read the reports. On account of the unnecessary delay in detection, the disease had ravaged all that came in the way of its relentless march. It had invaded the entire thickness of the bladder wall and there was stranding of the perivesical fat, which boded ill. Fear grasped my innards.

Instead of buckling under, I forced myself to work out the logistics. What was the further course of action, who was the best in this field, etc. I knew only one pompous urologist in my hospital. On asking around, I learnt that he probably got one cancer patient in three months, but Dr Arvind Soni (AS) at Sunder Sanyal Cancer Hospital (SSCH) was a uro-oncologist who probably did fifteen such cases in a day. I fixed up an appointment with Dr Soni for the very next day. I put the reports and our medical insurance papers in a bag and rang up the health insurance agent to ask how much we had at our disposal. He said that we were entitled to two and a half lakh rupees, plus a no-claim bonus of fifty thousand rupees – a pittance as far as cancer surgery went. To think that I had had to force MS even to buy this joint insurance! He agreed only when I said he and I could pay the premium every alternate year. The agent assured us that SSCH was in the panel of the insurance company. I asked if a cashless facility was available at the hospital. Though he said yes, I could sense the hesitancy in his voice. I let it pass, for that was the least of our worries; we had to proceed urgently whether we got the insurance money or not. The epitome of efficiency, I busied myself with practicalities to stop the emotional impact from hitting me.

I rang up Simar and told him that something really scary had occurred, but he was busy in a meeting and said he would call later. He never did, for he thought I was talking about a difficult case and he would get to hear of it sooner or later. A chef at a five-star hotel, he was serving his notice period before shifting to Bengaluru for a more lucrative offer. I also tried contacting Karan, my unmarried elder son, a liver specialist, in America, but could not get through. I thought he might be away on one of his many international trips because he was called to give talks all over the world. I did not want to tell my sister Ruby before my sons, or for that matter MS's sister Amrit (his only surviving sibling), who was so emotionally labile that she would be more of a liability than a help. We had more important things to do than to take care of her hysteria.

Having done all I could for the time being, I let open the floodgates, allowing a deluge of sorrow to submerge me.

2.3.13

There was no sleep for us that night and for many nights to come. MS had gone numb after reading the report and uttered not a word. The next morning, I got up with a heavy heart and began crying into my morning tea. I envisaged a long downhill struggle in the years ahead but was determined not to give up without a fight. It would be *my* fight against cancer. MS was but a trophy, a sorry one at that, we both were after.

MS snapped me out of my despondency with a stinging barb. *'Hun tu kyun ro rahi hai, batera time milega baad vich* (Why are you crying now, you'll get ample time to do so afterwards).' Before I could react, he disappeared into the bathroom. Strangled cries and huge sobs emanated from behind closed doors. It was indeed a sorry household where each individual retreated into a private hell to give vent to grief, instead of sharing the pain with each other.

However tumultuous the journey of our matrimony, whatever the companionship or lack of it, I could not remain indifferent to his pain. I rang up my sons again. This time I got both. I informed them about their father's reports and our impending visit to the cancer specialist. Leaving them to get over this shock, I drove MS to SSCH for the 9 a.m. appointment with Dr AS. MS began to cry on the way. Instead of consoling him, I told him in no-nonsense terms, 'The one major difference between the success of a treatment and its failure is the willpower of the individual. You give up on life and life gives up on you. Draw upon your inner reserves to persevere and you win.' This stemmed his flow of tears. I have this strange habit. Whatever my state of mind, a song befitting that emotion rises unbidden to my lips.

'You know which song I am humming under my breath now?' I asked MS. He did not answer but I continued, 'It is *Aa dekhein zara kisme kitna hai dum, jum ke rakhna kadam, mere saathiya* ... This will be our anthem henceforth and we'll fight it together.' Neither of us used the dreaded word 'cancer' ever.

I had been to SSCH a couple of times earlier to attend a few onco-gynae workshops but that was a long time ago. In the intervening decade a new building had been added, and the throng of miserables had increased to proportions befitting a government hospital, though it was an expensive private set-up. People broken in body and spirit crowded the corridors, driven by the tenuous force of hope. It catered to north India and beyond, for I saw people from Afghanistan, Nepal and even Africa. I had expected depressed faces set in expressions of resigned acceptance of impending doom or people crying, but they moved about with normal expressions on their faces. Patients who had lost their hair to chemotherapy walked past with heads covered with scarves or caps or blatantly exposed as if to thumb their nose at the disease. During my college days, residents with a macabre sense of humour had called the follow-up medical oncology clinics filled with bobbing bald heads 'coconut clinics'.

We got MS registered and I sent my card inside. We got no preferential treatment despite the fact that both of us were doctors. As MS's name had been spelt wrong, I sent him to correct the error lest it come in the way of his insurance claim. Just then, our turn came and I found myself facing a tall, swarthy, bespectacled Dr AS, who showed neither compassion nor concern. We were there just to add our lakhs to the crores he was minting. He gave us just two minutes of his time – so much for counselling a fresh cancer patient frightened out of his wits!

Going through the MRI and the CECT reports he asked, without looking up, 'Does he smoke?'

'He is a Sikh,' I retorted, stung to the quick. At this, he looked up for the first time to see MS, a turbaned Sikh with facial hair.

'We will do a TURBT, and if the bladder wall is involved, we will remove it.'

'MRI and CT show bladder wall involvement,' I said.

'They tend to over-diagnose.'

I sincerely hoped that it was so. Anyway, we needed a histopathology report for confirmation of the diagnosis and grading of the disease before deciding on further action.

MS was to be admitted the very next day, a Sunday, and the surgery was scheduled for Monday, but before that there were formalities to be completed. We trudged to the old building for a PAC (pre-anaesthetic check-up), where the anaesthetist examined MS, read his reports and referred him to the endocrinologist for his diabetes and to the cardiologist for his fascicular bundle branch block that showed up on the

ECG – mild in itself, but cardiology fitness was a prerequisite for surgery.

Simar called to say he could not concentrate on his work. He had taken off and was coming straight away. I told him not to rush as we were at the hospital and would remain there for a while. At this he decided to bring Mona and the baby along, as her parents went for satsang every weekend and there would be no one to help her with the baby. Packing their bags and getting them ready would take time and they would start by 4 p.m., which was fine by me.

It was amazing how priorities change. A few weeks earlier, I would have been overjoyed at having the baby back, but today all I could ask Simar was, 'But who will look after Mona and Jessy? We have our hands full.'

'She'll manage for a day; her parents will come tomorrow.'

MS's investigations were over by 4 p.m. and after an hour's rest he went to attend his clinic twelve kilometres away. As he was to get admitted the very next day, I told him to get his chequebook and whatever cash he kept there, for we would need it tomorrow. I withdrew my upper limit of forty thousand rupees from the ATM and collected whatever cash was lying at home and put it in my purse in case what MS had was insufficient.

I also rang up Simar to tell him not to come early as MS had gone to his clinic; hence there was no need for me to miss mine and I would be free only by 8 p.m. I also passed on the news of MS's illness and impending hospitalisation to my sister Ruby and MS's brother's son Paramjit in Nainital. Sadly, MS's brother, who would have been a great help, had expired some years back. Now the entire responsibility of MS's treatment fell upon me. Paramjit wanted to come immediately but I told him that Monday would be fine as he could alternate with Simar in keeping vigil by MS's bed night and day while I did the running around. Ruby had problems of her own involving the police and a court case, as the upper storey of their home was illegally occupied by land mafia, and she could not contribute her mite. I reassured her that it was fine.

I came home from work at 8.15 p.m. With nothing to distract me, MS's cancer began to prey on my mind. I would have liked to share my worries with Simar but when I called I learnt that they had made a stopover at Ruby's place. What hurt was the sound of laughter in the background. I overheard Ruby telling Mona, 'What fun we had that day –' She cut herself short when she realised that I was on the phone. Life went on as usual for others, as long as they were not personally hit. Lightning hadn't struck Ruby and Mona personally, but what about Simar! How could he join the revelry when his father had just been diagnosed with a dreadful disease?

That night, we played with Jessy as if there was no tomorrow. There was a flurry of photographs with MS, for time was running out and in the foreseeable future there would be one person less in our family photographs. I smiled valiantly through my tears.

3.3.13

The baby could not cheer MS up as I had hoped and I do not blame MS. There was the matter of his life and death to consider. After a few minutes with Jessy, he went to pack his bag; Simar went to help him. By 3 p.m. we were all set to go. I put fifty thousand rupees in my purse and asked MS to hand me his money, as the patient would be stripped of his personal clothes and belongings and I would be managing the admission, advance deposit, etc. To my utter amazement, he told me that he hadn't brought any.

'What about your chequebook?' I asked. 'Sign a few blank cheques in case we need the money urgently.'

He gave no answer. It dawned upon me that he had deliberately left it behind. That his miserliness could reach such pathological proportions was unbelievable! That he could stoop so low as to con me into paying for the life-threatening pathology in his body was beyond comprehension. With difficulty, I swallowed my anger.

I had read somewhere that the money you leave behind after you die is the extra hard work you have done to no gain. This had made a great impact on me and I had decided to spend my surplus money on a world tour. How was I to foresee that I would have to shell out major chunks for MS's cancer treatment, while he contributed not a penny. The ordeal had barely begun and I was already exhausted – mentally, physically and emotionally, and now the additional financial burden.

Simar drove us to the hospital after ardaas. The admission clerk demanded a deposit of sixty-five thousand rupees. The doctor had said that TURBT would cost sixty thousand rupees and they were asking for more at the very outset. I marched down to the accounts department and asked them to initiate formalities for a cashless facility, but it looked like people come to this place with bagsful of cash and the hospital had no intention of doing business on credit. With limited financial resources, poor insurance cover and no contribution from MS for his treatment, we opted for an economy room.

I asked for counselling facilities for a newly diagnosed case of cancer. I was shown an empty chair and desk in the busy open lounge, where people, chiefly cancer survivors, shared their positive experiences on working days. I would have thought that qualified professionals and privacy were of paramount importance to overcome the shock and find solace. Later I learnt that the hospital had a psychotherapy unit and the head of that department did meet MS days later – after major upheavals had already occurred. She left after a five-minute meeting with him, judging erroneously that he was taking the disease in his stride and did not need psychotherapy. Indeed! Appearances could be deceptive, but I left it at that.

I met the person in charge of room allotments. On learning that I was the head of the department of gynaecology in a corporate hospital, he gave us the best room in the circumstances, a secluded corner bed by a large glass window. It was air-conditioned and clean and overlooked a lush green lawn. A handsome Keralite nurse took MS's vitals, got his reports photocopied, drew blood for investigations and put him on insulin in view of the TURBT the next morning. I held MS's hand (something we had never done before) and together we listened to the shabad kirtan recorded on my cell phone. Simar had gone to explore the facility, as he would be staying back with his father for the night. I went home a while later as Mona and the baby were alone.

4.3.13

Paramjit couldn't bear to stay away any longer and had set out from Nainital. As people tend to do when needed most, our domestic help started acting smart. He was unmoved by the calamity that had befallen the household that provided his bread and butter. He was annoyed at being awakened early and packed my breakfast sullenly. I had to reach the hospital before 7 a.m. to wish MS luck before he was shifted to the OT. At the hospital we waited and waited and waited. No one gave us any information regarding the cause of the delay. By 2.40 p.m. I was ready to blow my top. MS was a diabetic and they had kept him on an empty stomach since morning. He could go into hypoglycaemic shock, which could kill him before the cancer. Only after I created a ruckus did the nursing staff contact the resident and start an IV line. If this was how they treated a doctor patient, that too in a private hospital, I shuddered to think of the plight of the cancer-stressed public in government hospitals.

As I, too, was a diabetic, I had my leftover breakfast of mooli paratha with coffee that Simar brought from the cafeteria downstairs. I was so depleted by the stress, the interminable wait and the lack of sleep that I fell asleep on the hard, narrow bench by MS's bedside. The call finally came at 4.30 p.m. Simar and I went along with MS's stretcher, as they do in films, and left him outside the OT door. With such a large turnover, the protocol in SSCH was that the bed vacated by the patient shifted to the OT was immediately allocated to the patient who had come out of the OT after surgery! So we packed our meagre belongings and shifted to a seedy waiting area with collapsible benches that one had to grab and occupy till such time our patients were in the OT or ICU. These could be opened at night and the lucky ones could grab some sleep during nightlong vigils. It looked like a sordid, crowded railway waiting area. In one corner was a TV on silent mode, which the introverts watched silently, while the gregarious ones exchanged cancer notes, voiced their opinion about the doctors, the disease and the hospital. The telephone near the door was distracting. Each time it rang there was utter silence as the guard picked it up and called out the name of the patient whose relatives were called. It reminded me of John Donne's lines:

> Therefore, send not to know
> For whom the bell tolls,
> It tolls for thee.

Ruby and her husband came to look us up at the hospital and were a welcome distraction. The phone rang for us in their presence. The operation was over and we were called to interact with MS before he was shifted to the surgical ICU across the corridor. The doctor was brief and curt, unapologetic about the delay. They had taken multiple biopsies and were awaiting the results before taking any decisions. With such a large turnover the histopathology reports in this hospital came within twenty-four hours as opposed to the week or so it took in other hospitals. All we could do was pray and keep our fingers crossed.

5.3.13

It took a cancer for MS to appreciate my worth; it took a cancer for me to overlook his faults that included grave ones like neglect during my ICU admissions, once for a near-fatal head injury after a fall and the second time for an acute attack of breathlessness due to laryngeal spasm. This was not the time to settle scores. Grudges were washed away with tears through which I smiled and held his hands to cheer him up. Even if I did not love him, MS was family, as his mother had been. I had nursed her through Alzheimer's and a broken hip for two long years, until her death in 2000. No matter what, I would do whatever it took to make his life comfortable till the end of life – his or mine, whichever came first. After all, I was a full-fledged case of metabolic syndrome and could very well succumb to a sudden heart attack (as people were wont to on my side of the family), while the cancer was still at it, eating him up bit by bit.

The next day, I took Paramjit to meet MS in the ICU during the half-hour visiting time between 8 a.m. and 8.30 a.m. allowed for relatives to meet the patient. At 2 p.m. I went again with Simar to meet Dr AS to decide the further course of action. Though he saw us standing outside, he offered neither sympathy nor a chair. He was totally lacking in the courtesy that one doctor shows another. We were equal in designation too – I was the HOD (Obs & Gynae) at a corporate hospital and he was the Urogynae Cancer in-charge here – though he earned more from one case than I earned in a month.

As I was chafing at this slight, wonder of wonders, Sister Catherine came like an angel in my line of vision. I latched on to her as to a lifeline in this callous, indifferent place where the stricken received no sympathy. She had been the OT in-charge in my hospital earlier and was now the OT supervisor here. I flung myself in her arms and began to cry. When she learnt the reason of my visit, there was genuine sympathy in her eyes. She introduced me to the ICU staff as her ma'am, upon which they looked at me with new respect. She offered me a chair and, as soon as the patient inside Dr AS's chamber left, took me to him. Now he was cordial and even managed a smile or two. However, the news he gave was sinister – the tumour was malignant and invasive. The flimsy citadel of false hope crumbled to dust. The surgery would be major – radical cystectomy, which involved removal of the bladder, seminal vesicles, prostate and regional lymph, with the formation of a neo-ileal bladder (part of the intestines would be used to create a new bladder). This was a relatively new procedure and was done so that the patient would be able to urinate from his natural passage, the urethra, and not into a bag through a hole in the abdominal wall. He asked me if I would like an open or robotic surgery. The cost in eco would be three lakh rupees plus another seventy thousand rupees for medicines. The five-year survival rate was 65–70 per cent.

I said I would have to consult my brothers and son abroad and, emboldened by Sister Catherine's presence, asked him the reason for the delay yesterday. He said that one of the

OTs had to be shut down for repair work and a major surgery took a lot more time than anticipated due to complications. 'The least you could have done was inform us,' I wanted to say but let it be.

Simar insisted that I do not miss work to be by MS's bedside. It would only keep me brooding. I had much on my plate already, looking into matters that were urgent, like arranging the finance and taking a second and maybe third opinion from other oncologists before deciding what was best for my husband. As for sitting with MS, Simar and Paramjit took turns. I also researched extensively online to gather information and was amazed at MS's lack of desire to learn more about his condition. Maybe he was in a state of denial and did not want to discuss his future, or rather, the lack of it.

When I went back at 4.30 p.m., MS had been shifted out of the ICU. The bed he got this time was in the middle of a stuffy, overcrowded ward. But I was cheered by the scene being enacted by his bedside. Sister Catherine, the diminutive Christian from Kerala, was telling the Tibetan nurse in charge of the ward that MS (a Sikh) was a relative and she better look after him well! God bless her. We tried getting a better room but the hospital was full.

Relatives rang up from all over India and abroad, not giving me a moment's rest. Of all the conflicting advice I got, one made sense. A PET scan should be done for surgery to look for distant metastasis. What would be the use of such an extensive, mutilating surgery if there were mets all over? I was surprised that the money-minting machine Dr AS did not suggest it himself. When I tentatively asked his opinion, he said that they usually did not do a PET (which was strange), but if we wanted it, we could get it done today as the surgery was scheduled for the next day. Paramjit stayed back for the night, while Simar, who had been at the hospital since Sunday evening, came home with me.

On the way back, we discussed MS's condition and the problem Ruby and her husband were facing. Ruby's grandson had developed renal problems and their entire family was in a state of panic. As for the 'illegal' occupants of the upper storey of their house, it turned out that they were 'legal' occupants as her husband MH's brother had sold them *his* share illegally, which he could not without consent, and MH wasn't even aware of the transaction. Matters had come to blows leading to police involvement and a court case. Simar said that we should not leave this sort of mess behind for him and his brother. I assured him I would sort out everything before I died, but what about the duty of children towards their parents?

'How do you and your brother intend to help your father, who is not shelling out a paisa for his own treatment?' I asked.

At this he kept quiet, though he did contribute one lakh rupees later.

As promised, I made a detailed will a few days later and got it witnessed by two people, though I knew that I could always change it at my discretion if my children did not live up to my expectations. I tried to share it to MS a few months later but he showed no interest lest he too be induced to do the same!

6.3.13

Cancer was a great leveller. People from most of north India and other countries too converged at one place with one aim – to beat the hell out of cancer. Some succeeded; some lost. If the light-eyed Afghani boy sitting on the seat across mine cries, I cry too, for we are suffering the same helpless pain over the irrevocable, unwanted change occurring in our lives and the terrible fear it brings along. Why, even now I could easily die of a heart attack before MS, but the possibility did not hang over my head like MS's cancer did, and thereby it evoked no terror.

My thoughts turned to Punjab, my beautiful, green, fertile land of plenty. It was being ravaged by drugs and cancer. Every family had a drug addict and a cancer patient. The dark, rich earth yielded bumper crops after the Green Revolution and overnight the farmers found themselves rich beyond imagination, but the gold their land yielded brought them no joy these days. The aimless youth squandered their fathers' fortunes on cheap titillation like porn and drugs, which destroyed them and devastated their families. The nexus that was turning the state into a drug haven had dug its claws deeper than cancer, for peddlers from across the border to the highest police officials and politicians were involved in this lucrative business and had little incentive to stop it. As for the cancer rampant in the state, it was paradoxically agriculture which had blessed them with riches that cursed them with terrible deaths. Carcinogenic fertilisers and pesticides leached into their lands, underground water, wells, grass, cow milk, their very blood and bones. People sold their lands and homes sighting a glimmer of hope, which would be snuffed out sooner or later. Entire trainloads of cancer patients went to Bikaner for chemotherapy in the morning and returned in the evening. Colloquially called the 'cancer train', it offered free travel for cancer patients and a chaperone. Tiny tots too were not spared. Parents watched with helpless agony as their little one succumbed to the deadly disease, while his older sibling lolled about in a drugged stupor. In SSCH too the children's cancer ward was filled with patients, chiefly from Punjab. I recalled reading an article long ago that said when cancer-afflicted children died their parents felt guilty because they were not as grief-stricken as they ought to have been. But this was because they had done all the grieving possible during the prolonged illness and were relieved when the ordeal was finally over.

I am a doctor, but now as a patient's relative I could see that patients' grouses weren't entirely baseless. However, I had always been compassionate and sensitive to their needs. Even in my Lady Hardinge days, a hospital whose patients were the illiterate and poor, I never ill-treated women in labour, as most others did. As it is they were suffering enough and did not need rude hospital staff to add to their woes. Some cruel nurses even slapped their thighs open during delivery and taunted '*Aadmi ke neeche padke mazey leti hai, ab dard bhi bardasht kar; chilla mat* (If you can enjoy yourself lying under a man, you can take the pains too, so don't shout).' Even in private practice I never overcharged or did operations that were not necessary and slept soundly each night with a clear conscience. Despite his many faults, MS too never overcharged his patients. In fact, his professional fees were a laughable pittance, for he was entirely unambitious. Now his doctor was about to perform an extensive, expensive surgery on him without a PET scan. We had to literally beg Dr AS to allow it. If MS had secondaries that were at inoperable sites, the severe physical, mental and financial trauma would be in vain. But even as I was consulting doctors in my family abroad and other oncologists before deciding whether to go ahead with the relatively new robotic surgery or opt for the time-tested open surgery, Dr AS went ahead and planned for robotic surgery without even a by-your-leave. I complied meekly because the other doctors I had consulted gave conflicting advice. During the rounds, my husband's doctor barely gave us two minutes of his time, leaving me highly unsatisfied after each visit.

There were other new experiences too. I'd eat with the other patients' relatives in the park, enjoying the pleasant winter sun, stretch out on a stone bench and get a free spa treatment which eased the ache in my back. I had never imagined that I, a senior consultant, would lie thus in an open public place, but I couldn't care less.

As I was basking in the sun there appeared behind my right ear an intense itch, a sure sign of lice infestation, something I had never suffered since the age of nine! I guess I had picked it up from the folding bench in the waiting room. A few hours later, the itch became so severe that I was ready to scratch my scalp off. I rushed to get the appropriate medicated lotion and rubbed it vigorously on my scalp right there to obtain blessed relief. A refreshing shampoo after 24 hours and I was as good as new. After that, whenever I felt the need to rest I did so on the sun-sterilised stone benches in the hospital garden, avoiding the uncomfortable benches of the seedy waiting room.

When I re-entered the ward after lunch, I heard heart-wrenching screams and felt sorry for the person suffering such agonies. And then I realised it was MS. I had never heard him scream before and could not associate the horrific sounds with him. He had suffered a bad night, for his catheter had repeatedly got blocked with blood clots, causing painful obstruction to the flow of urine. The treatment of this complication, a bladder wash, was far more painful. But it was blocked again and only after repeated appeals could Paramjit, who had stayed the night with MS, persuade the staff to come for another bladder wash. No wonder the curtains around his bed were drawn, though that offered precious little privacy in a ward bustling with very sick patients and a staff sensitised to human misery. I waited as they performed the painful procedure, trying to shut my ears against the terrifying cries. Later, holding the hand of a wan and drained MS, I tried to lift his spirits even as mine were sinking. His urine bag contained more blood and less urine, perhaps due to the procedure.

MS's PET scan was being done today and on Simar fell the responsibility of wheeling him from one place to another, such was the shortage of staff. A while later we were told verbally that there were no metastases. Even as I was thanking God for small mercies, MS was called again. Our hearts sank but they wanted him only for a delayed film, which again revealed the same findings. Included in the preoperative formalities was arranging for MS's rare O negative blood. The blood bank was in the basement and Simar and Paramjit donated blood. They would not take mine as I was above the age limit. Even as we were wondering from where we would get another donor, we found an angel in the depths of this dungeon. God had specifically placed her there for the few months we needed her. She was Malvika, a kind young doctor, who was also the wife of Simar's colleague. She was on a rotary posting in the pathology department that was situated next to the blood bank. When I asked Malvika to find out if their blood bank had O negative blood, she said, 'Aunty, one donor is standing right in front of you.'

Good souls like Malvika and Catherine breathed the same air as the demons that destroyed the trust placed in them. There were rumours of a caucus of unscrupulous doctors whose modus operandi was as follows: the pathologists gave a cancer positive report for a cancer negative specimen. Scared out of their wits, consent for radical surgery was readily given and the pathologist got a hefty cut from the fees charged by the oncosurgeon. Not only were patients being put through unnecessary surgery, they were subjected to a lifelong dread of recurrence. Others were glad that their 'disease' was caught early and they 'survived' to live a cancer-free life and died years later of other causes. As for these unprincipled caregivers, they received accolades for such high post-surgery survival rates! When I voiced my fears to Malvika, she took the TURBT tissue slides to the departmental head and got them re-examined under the microscope in front of her own eyes. Though she assured us that the report was genuine, it was ominous – high-grade uro-epithelial malignancy invading the musculature of the bladder wall.

Finally, all was set for surgery. Mamaji, a very senior cardiologist, came to cheer us up before the ordeal. Being deeply religious, he told us to repose complete faith in God, though He had not been kind to my uncle. I had seen his wife succumb slowly, relentlessly to pancreatic cancer. I remembered her tall, gaunt form sitting in their drawing room with an IV line in her arm, begging me to kill her. I could only avert my eyes in horror. She eventually died after a large blood vomit.

7.3.13

It had now become a habit to wake up with a heavy heart and decrease the burden somewhat by crying into my morning tea. I got up at an unearthly hour to reach the hospital in time so that I could meet MS before he was shifted to the OT for his marathon surgery. As I would be keeping vigil for hours in the hospital premises, I woke up Vijay so that he could pack my food. I suffered from IBS (irritable bowel syndrome) and avoided eating outside. Moreover, I was a diabetic and it was good to have something handy in case hypoglycaemia set in. He began to grumble. The last thing I wanted was a disgruntled servant during this phase of our lives. I tried telling him that we were going through stressful times and I would compensate him for the inconvenience.

'*Aisi naukri ko laat marta hoon* (I kick such a job),' he replied.

At this, I broke down and began to howl and cry right there in front of Paramjit and that heartless creep. I drove off to the hospital without a word. This set a precedent and he began to think that he could get away with anything. When Paramjit and I returned from the hospital one day at 4 p.m., hungry, thirsty, exhausted and depressed, there was no food on the table and no help in the house. He just didn't care.

During the period of MS's hospitalisation, I tried to compensate Vijay for waking him early by allowing him two hours' sleep in the afternoon. That is why when a woman came asking for him at 3 p.m., I told her that he was resting. He had heard our conversation from his room on the second floor and rushed down to meet her. I learnt that he was a rampant womaniser and she was one of his paramours! He wanted me to allow her to stay with him in my house if I wanted his services.

'Definitely not at this cost!' I exclaimed, outraged.

Unprepared for this outburst, he played his trump card.

'Then I will leave your services today itself.'

'Why today, get lost now!' There was just so much a person could take.

I could keep a part-time maid and, if necessary, buy food from outside. It's just that I was so preoccupied and stressed out that I had neither the time nor the inclination to look for new help and teach him the functioning of my household. I had also learnt that Vijay planned to go to his village in a month's time and had vacated his rented quarters in Shakurpur, where he took his lovers and hid the things he pilfered. If he left now, he would neither get another job nor a place to keep his belongings for such a short time. This put him in a spot. During the month I had gained, I would find and train another domestic help, and I hoped MS would have recovered from his mammoth surgery by then.

Vijay was stumped, for he had expected me to plead with him to stay. Instead, I spewed the venom I had bottled for so long.

'Tune mare hue ko maara hai, isse badi haivaniyat kya ho sakti hai (You have killed the dying, what could be more demonic that this)? You made me cry on the day of my husband's cancer surgery and did not even have the decency to say sorry. I can never forgive you for that,' I said.

Contrite, he begged forgiveness. After making him grovel till I felt vindicated, I relented, for now the equation had changed.

This time Dr AS had promised to take up MS's case first, as it would be a very long one. Our doctor lived up to his reputation and delayed MS's 7 a.m. surgery indefinitely, without informing us. On tenterhooks, we paced up and down. Morbid thoughts and pre-operative preparation including a bowel wash had kept MS up for the better part of the night. He was finally called upstairs at 11 a.m. We sent him on his way with our best wishes and heartfelt prayers.

The operation began at 12.35 p.m. Barely had we settled in the waiting area when from the loudspeaker came the ominous announcement that MS's relatives were to go to the OT. Fearing the worst, we rushed upstairs only to learn that the mercenaries wanted to know if we had deposited the cash. Of course we had, but I could not locate the receipt in my bag. Thinking that I had forgotten it at home, I went back to look for it while Simar and Paramjit stayed put. Simar rang me up sometime later to tell me that they had found it among MS's papers but wanted me to get some more cash as a reserve. As we were talking on the phone, I heard another announcement for MS's relatives on the harsh, railway-platform-like loudspeaker in the background. It turned out that they wanted us to buy a urobag. I could not believe it! Did they have to frighten us to death for such a small thing? They could have easily used one from the OT and added the cost to our bill.

Ruby brought lunch and sat with us during the long, weary vigil. The operation ended at 8 p.m. Despite the dread of being reinfected with lice, I was glad to grab a chair-cum-bed in the waiting area to straighten my aching back. It was an uncomfortable contraption made of white-painted iron with three cushioned seats covered with green rexine. We spent the time swapping stories and swatting and waving off mosquitoes, as we waited tensely.

We went to the OT to meet MS as he was being transferred to the ICU across the corridor. He had tubes coming out of every orifice, natural and artificial. Like in the movies, he groggily enquired, '*Main kahaan hoon* (Where am I)?' and asked for Sister Catherine! I pretended to be highly offended as he hadn't asked for me. Perhaps she was the last person he had seen before the anaesthesia kicked in.

When Ruby's husband MH came to pick her up, he said if I needed anything, I should ask him without hesitation. I demurred politely. The next day when he mouthed the same inanity, I thought he meant it. I had some money in SBI near his factory and asked his help to get the money transferred to the SBI bank near my house. I would give him a letter of authority and he would have to do some paperwork.

'*Bas yahi kaam reh gaya* (As if this is all the work I have left to do),' he said under his breath. This, when he owed me big time!

Though everyone, especially my sister and mother, had vociferously opposed my relationship with Rajan, they had no compunctions going to him for help. He had contacts in all departments, legal and illegal, and knew how to get things done. When MH was in trouble over the illegal sale of his house, he had asked me to arrange a meeting with Rajan and since then, Rajan, who thrived on making me and mine (especially those who had hated his guts) beholden to him, had been helping them with the police and the court case while Ruby, now that they needed his help, took to treating him to him lavish repasts whenever he came to their house to 'discuss' their business.

Where was the issue of propriety now? Ruby soothed her conscience by saying that her husband had sought Rajan's help when she was in the US babysitting her son's newborn. She insisted that MH did not know about my relationship with Rajan and she was doing me a favour by hiding it from him. This was difficult to believe, for the entire clan knew. Moreover, I cared two hoots for his opinion anyways, especially when there had been a distinct cooling of relations between Rajan and me. I hated to be beholden to him for my self-righteous family which had disgraced me on this account but had no qualms about taking his help.

So this was how life was going to be from now on – bullied by helps, slighted by relatives, bossed by one son (Simar had become overbearing) and neglected by the other. 'This is what happens to a woman when she is left to fend for herself. This is how I will be treated by all and sundry when he is no more,' I thought, drowning in self-pity.

Just then, as if on cue, the raagi on the kirtan tape I had put on in the car stereo sang *la vadani aas* (stop expecting from others – and ask for whatever you want only from the One above). In retrospect, MS had never been a help; even when he was well, I had to fend for myself.

8.3.13

I visited MS in the ICU during the visiting hours. He appeared to be doing well and called the nurses angels. While the other patients in the ICU were either groaning or deeply sedated, I learnt that MS had asked for his specs and the morning newspaper! I felt a reluctant admiration for the man creep in. At this rate, I hoped, he would recover soon.

As Paramjit would remain in the waiting area, I left for work and performed a difficult hysterectomy. Completely drained, physically and emotionally, I lay down for my power nap after lunch. My head felt like a block of wood. True to form, even from that distance, on his first post-operative day, MS found a way to disturb me, as he had done all along. The ICU nurse rang me up at the very moment I had fallen asleep with a message from MS. He wanted me to bring his patka, the head cover that Sikhs wear when not wearing a turban, when I came for my evening visit. I felt like patkofying (slamming) his head or mine against a wall!

9.3.13

The next morning I found MS reading the papers with his patka and specs in the ICU as if it was a normal day at home. He had been in pain last night but his spirits were not dampened. Remarkable was his resilience. When the male nurse came to take him for a walk around the ICU to prevent clot formation, MS insisted on taking two rounds of the ICU instead of the mandatory one. I was glad that he was not a fussy patient and was bent on getting well soon. Later, when he graduated to walking in the hospital corridor, I would accompany him for his morning walk in our unusual 'park' and joke, 'Now you will have to keep pace with me.'

He had a habit of walking ahead of me without a backward glance, which was a hazard to my safety at times. Especially when we walked through the Shakurpur slum (notorious for its pickpockets and eve-teasers) towards the Samrat cinema hall every Sunday evening. His standard refrain then was, 'I cannot walk slowly.' And now …

After the walk, the nursing attendant would tap his upper back to dislodge any phlegm collected there, rub it vigorously with powder to prevent bedsores and lay him down in a reclining position. It was time now for MS to exercise his lungs with the help of a spirometer – a device into which he had to blow so that the three coloured balls at the bottom were pushed up with each breath. Try as he might, he could only blow two of the three balls up. Simar and I would laugh up our sleeves as we urged him to blow harder knowing full well that the piece was defective and the third ball could not rise!

I went to the bank where my father had opened an account jointly with me; it had about three lakh in fixed deposits. I bore no grudge against my father for leaving prime properties and crores in cash to his sons, but the cumbersome process of retrieving this paltry sum bugged me. There was a lot of red tape involved – depositing a copy of his death certificate, deleting his name from the account, dissolving the FDs, filling the transfer form, etc., which made me vow not to make my children's inheritance so complicated.

The formalities over, I negotiated the traffic snarls to attend OPD and reached home at 3.30 p.m. exhausted. There were endless phone calls to attend to. MS's sister agonised over her brother's plight long distance. I had expressly forbidden her to come, for we had enough on our hands already and I was not up to dealing with her hysterics. During her mother's decline into Alzheimer's, she would fly all the way from Bengaluru, but instead of helping us care for her mother, all she did was cry.

As the morning traffic jam had been excruciating, I took the metro and then rickshaw for my half-hour date with my husband in the ICU and found this mode of transport to be far more cumbersome. I felt ashamed of cribbing about my minor discomforts after seeing MS pinned to his bed with six tubes attached to his body. There was the CVP line from his neck vein, an IV line on his arm, a Ryle's tube thrust down his nose right up to his stomach, a catheter up his urethra and a supra-pubic catheter in the new bladder made out of a part of his intestines that they had partially detached. There was a thick plastic drain from a puncture in his abdominal wall that collected blood and serosanguinous fluid from the raw area left after so extensive a surgery in his abdominal cavity. Stoically he bore his sufferings and even had it in him to give me a wan smile when I entered the ICU.

Simar and Paramjit were doing a good job, taking turns to keep vigil night and day. As for me, having schooled myself to be strong, I had stopped crying, but stress began to manifest in the form of severe migraines that returned with a vengeance, after years.

10.3.13

A harrowing nine days have passed. MS suffered from painful gaseous distension twice the previous night and was given the injection Aciloc. Thankfully, he could feel the gas moving now. After visiting him in the evening I went with Paramjit to watch *Kai Po Che*. It was a nice movie, but I felt guilty about indulging in such pleasures while MS lay in pain in the ICU, more so when his sister called in the middle of the movie and I had to ward her off with a fib. Why this unnecessary guilt? I was doing my best by her brother and desperately needed something to distract me from our ordeal.

11.3.13

MS was feeling very weak. His haemoglobin levels dropped from the preoperative 13 g/dL to 7 g/dL despite the blood transfusions, perhaps due to the leakage from various tubes. He received two packed blood cells that day and could not be shifted out of the ICU as planned.

This was disturbing. Why, even his post-operative haemoglobin had been 9.8 g/dL, which was expected after the extensive robotic radical cystectomy surgery. Dr AS had done the maximum number of robotic surgeries in India and was quite skilled, which was why we had come to him in the first place (that it had converted him into an unfeeling robot too was a different matter). Another reason for selecting him and the place was because it was close to home, which was important considering the number of times in a day we had to come here to visit MS and the follow-up visits that MS would have to make as long as he lived.

Medicines worth ten to fifteen thousand rupees had to be purchased every day and money flowed like water. Also, the greater the number of days MS spent in the ICU, the more would be the expenditure. I also had to take care of the routine household expenditure such as for groceries and the electricity and water bills that otherwise was MS's responsibility. Of our combined expenses, he had offered to pick the tab for medicines, but when my diseases began increasing – hyperlipidaemia, diabetes and hypertension – my pharmacy bills piled up, and he coolly told me to buy my own medicines. Though I was quite capable of doing so and started buying them from that day onward years ago, what hurt was how little he cared about me. It was always about money, his money to be precise.

The smartass knew that I would not fail in my duty towards him though he had failed me repeatedly. During our long married life I had found him sadly wanting in both compassion and care. When I suffered a head injury after a fall down the broken stairs of my hospital, I had got eight stitches on my bleeding scalp and undergone CT scan by the time he arrived. As my relative, instead of staying by my side to watch for signs of internal bleeding like restlessness, confusion, coma, he went home and slept.

When I had to be nebulised in the ICU for laryngeal spasm after a severe bout of allergic cough, he did not rush to my side from his clinic. Instead, he first went home for lunch, past the hospital where I was, and was waiting in a queue to fill petrol at the pump when I rang him up again. Our home was just a kilometre away and he could have done this later. Incensed beyond words, I drove myself home, though I had been prohibited to do so. I also remember a time when I was on IV fluids for dehydration following a severe bout of gastroenteritis and he left me for his clinic. Though I was weak and sleepy, I had to keep awake to ring the bell for the nurse to change the bottle before it was completely empty, lest I die of air embolism. Each time, I suffered twice over – with the disease and by his callousness. In a fit of anger, I had once told him, 'If you think, despite being a husband and doctor, it is all right to neglect a seriously ill wife, I will remember it when you fall ill.' He was as strong as a horse in those days and rarely fell ill. At this he said, '*Tu te chandi hai ki main beemar pava* (You want me to fall ill),' which was untrue, but I wanted to give him a dose of his own medicine at least once in his lifetime. Now that an opportunity had come up, I could not bring myself to do so.

12.3.13

My morale sank to dismal depths after the final histopathology report. Out of the 22 lymph nodes removed, 6 were positive for cancer! This made it stage four cancer with barely 20–30 per cent five-year survival rate. I was in my office when Malvika gave me the news on the phone. I put my head down and my tears pooled on the wooden table.

I did not tell MS about the positive lymph nodes. The gaseous distension persisted, causing him a lot of distress. His intestines had been tampered with to fashion a new bladder; in retaliation, they had gone on strike. There were no bowel sounds and the Ryle's tube had to be reinserted.

13.3.13

The hospital bills mounted alarmingly and I was at my wits' end. In desperation, I met Dr AS to discuss MS's worsening condition and the increasing costs. He had given us an estimate of a little over four lakh rupees but already it had gone past five lakh. He curtly told me he had no say in the matter, and that was that. Each day I would hand Simar or Paramjit fifteen thousand rupees for medicines and it would vanish without a trace. Still, MS was neither out of danger nor out of the ICU.

Just as I was wondering what to do, Karan e-transferred ten thousand dollars in my name for his father's treatment! This eased my financial tension considerably and restored my faith in Karan, for I had begun to believe that he was failing in his filial duty. Simar helped by being around when he was needed most and had contributed one lakh rupees. Paramjit added his mite. Friendly by nature, he interacted with the guards and other patients' relatives and learnt that most of them bought medicines from outside at 40 per cent discount, when the hospital chemist gave us 20 per cent discount. In fact, only those with corporate mediclaim policies bought medicines from the hospital chemist as they could get the cost reimbursed. That the hospital chemist could afford to pay one lakh rupees rent per month meant that he was minting money. Not only were the medicines from the outside shops genuine and cheap, for the hospital accepted them, the kind chemists, to our mutual benefit, plied free rickshaws to and fro. This saved us at least four thousand rupees per day, for Paramjit got them for nine thousand rupees instead of the thirteen thousand rupees he had paid earlier. God bless him.

14.3.13

In time, everyone would depart, and it would be just MS and me and the cancer between us. After all, how long could Simar stay? He had to leave for his new job in Bengaluru sooner than later. Paramjit could not neglect his shop in Nainital indefinitely. It was being managed quite inefficiently by his mother these days. Mind-boggling was the enormity of my responsibility. Though MS was the one in pain, his illness was the cross I would have to bear, a cross he would not have borne had I been the one suffering from cancer. Along with everyone else, he would have smugly thought of it as my just deserts – retribution for the 'sin' of falling in love with another man while married to him.

MS's condition was still precarious, for the paralytic ileus persisted and his bowel sounds had not returned. To allow his intestines to recover from the operative assault, MS was only on IV fluids and was weakening day by day. I began to fear he could die due to a surgical complication. I was prepared to take on the prolonged, painful consequences of cancer, but this was unbearable. I broke down when his sister rang up. I let her speak with him. Suddenly the irony of the situation hit me and I smiled through my tears. I was praying that MS would belch and/or fart (that proclaimed that his intestines had started working again), the two things about which he had always been so uncivilised during our entire married life!

Curiously, all the things I hated in this man were the ones I longed for now. The one thing I wanted from MS today was not a thank you (which he never said once in all his remaining life) but a smelly fart, a trumpet that would announce the end of his intestines' strike!

The kindly ICU resident allowed me to sit inside the ICU way beyond visiting time as I was determined to meet Dr AS before I left. He came at 10 a.m. and answered my queries in unsatisfactory monosyllables. I showed him the HPE report.

'He will need chemotherapy six to eight weeks after surgery,' was all he said. 'That is, if he survives the complications of your surgery,' I wanted to say, but dared not. The immediate hurdle was paralytic ileus, which appeared insurmountable.

The ICU of a cancer hospital is the most cheerless place on earth. For the staff, it is just a job, a lucrative one at that, and it is easy to become immune to the sea of suffering humanity. We were not the only travel-weary people on this dismal jetty waiting for ships to take us or ours to 'Destination Death'. The collective fears and tears of patients and their relatives was a palpable presence that hung like a pall over our heads. It clutched hearts and eroded hope. Paramjit cried at the plight of an old couple who would lug heavy bags of medicines (which he took to carrying for them) for their only son, blind and cancer-ridden, lying in the ICU. Thankfully he obtained deliverance a few days later.

The OPDs, OTs, wards and the hands of oncologists were always full. The chances of litigation against them were minimal, for people come expecting adverse outcomes and are pleasantly surprised when cancer survivors go on to live long, productive lives. One oncosurgeon was callous enough to state that even if he inadvertently cut a major nerve resulting in paralysis of a particular part, he could always say that they had had to remove it due to cancer infiltration! Only once did I hear a paediatric medical oncologist state that she dreaded the visits of a little child with a horrifying cancerous tumour behind his right eye. Despite chemotherapy, it kept pushing the eye out of its socket! There was nothing they could do about it but await a merciful death!

In my branch of medicine (Obs and Gynae), the suffering I witnessed ended in tender joy. It was a joy to watch the look of ecstasy on the face of parents as they looked in wonder at their newborn after the ordeal of labour. However, litigation rates were high for our patients were largely healthy young women and the smallest untoward incident was unacceptable.

15.3.13

MS was finally shifted out of the ICU, though his abdomen appeared distended to me. We chose a corner bed in economy special, which cost about six hundred rupees more than the general ward but was much better. MS was happy with the place and the TV.

In the evening it was Paramjit's turn to be with MS and Simar returned home exhausted and irritable. Frayed nerves led to conflict. He found fault with everything, took offence at every little thing and rebuked me harshly when I forgot words or repeated something, as one is wont to do at this age, especially in such trying circumstances. The last thing I wanted was a showdown with my son, but I had had enough and gave him a piece of my mind.

16.3.13

A doctor at my hospital knew a surgeon in SSCH, who visited MS at his behest. Supine and erect abdominal X-rays were taken to rule out obstruction for which another surgery would be required in this weakened state. Thankfully there was none. His intestines were still on strike at the manhandling and would take their own sweet time to function. All we could do was bide time – which was ten days in MS's case. The doctor's fault lay in starting oral feeds before the intestines had fully recovered.

The medicine bills mounted, and though I gave them enough, I was not getting any money back from either of the two boys looking after MS. I became stricter about keeping expenditure records (I needed medicine bills anyway to claim reimbursement) including McDonald's, Haldiram's and butter chicken in Paramjit's case! Both had expressly refused home food and this added to the expense. Though they deserved this much leeway for their untiring vigil night and day by MS's bedside, I needed to know where my hard-earned money went. After this, they began handing the remaining money to the next on duty.

17.3.13

Mona and Jessy had long gone back to South Delhi, where she could stay with her parents. It mattered not a whit to me at this point. I did not have the time and energy to look after them, but her parents had matters of their own to sort out, and Simar was bringing mother and child back here.

The money Karan had sent was already used up and financial issues always lurked at the back of my mind. Bills, bills and more bills were all I got these days. The breaking point came when I had to pay MS's income tax returns from my pocket. As Simar was bringing his family back today, I asked him to stop by at the clinic and get MS's chequebook. When confronted thus by both mother and son, MS had no option but to tell us where he kept his clinic keys. Till now, his cupboard had been solely his and I had no access to it. The next time I was alone with MS I told him that the expenses were proving too much for me. If he had some cash stashed away at home (which I knew he had) he could tell me. At this he made a bone-chilling statement. 'Don't worry, when worst comes to worst, I will help you out of your predicament by opting out!' I never asked him for money again.

19.3.13

As I had dreaded all along, it was time for Simar and Paramjit to leave. Paramjit's mother had hit her head against a wall and hurt herself badly, so he had to leave. As for Simar, he could no longer postpone winding up before shifting base to Bengaluru. He took with him an efficient old help, Sauruv, who had just returned from his village, and went through the backbreaking task of packing for his shift to a prestigious upcoming hotel. They had bought him out of his parent company by paying half the money for his three-month notice period so that they would relieve him earlier. This one and a half months he could have served was spent looking after his father in the hospital. This meant he had to pay his company the remaining money from his own pocket.

There was no one to stay with MS that night, for I had to help Mona manage Jessy. Luckily, Reena, MS's late elder sister's daughter, had come from Chandigarh to look up her uncle and stayed with him at the hospital for a full twenty-four hours. I took a hot lunch for her in the afternoon and we updated each other on our affairs during that long lazy afternoon while MS snored under the effect of sedation.

Leaving Reena 'on duty' with her uncle, I returned to my evening clinic, after which I took Mona and Jessy to Dilli Haat for the Bihar Utsav. We indulged in retail therapy; she bought Madhubani paintings made by an award-winning artist for her new home in Bengaluru, while I bought a Bhagalpuri silk sari with a Madhubani painting of a scene from the Ramayana along its pallu and border at a bargain price of five thousand three hundred rupees. Subconsciously I chose a pastel shade, keeping in mind my impending widowhood. So heady was the brief respite that we thought nothing of placing my precious two-month-old grandson on a camel's back and clicking pictures. It was so much fun after the gloomy time spent at the hospital and fun was what I needed badly to raise my spirits.

20.3.13

Though MS's Aadhaar card had arrived by post a long time ago, mine got lost on the way. As this was an important document, without which no official transaction would be possible, I had reapplied and was to collect it from the office today. Though I had reached way before office time, there was a long queue ahead of me. The office was on the second floor and I found myself standing in a line on the first floor. Within minutes, the queue behind me had snaked down to the ground floor. When the office finally opened, to my dismay I got token no 68! This meant I would be spending the entire morning on these dingy steps.

I nostalgically thought of Rajan, with whom I still maintained a tenuous, chiefly telephonic relationship. On an impulse I rang him up. He told me to hand over the phone to the person in charge. I do not know what transpired between the two, but within minutes I found myself being ushered to the front of the line. After the biometrics were done, I went to a cell phone repair centre to get my phone formatted, for it was impossible to do without one. Exhausted by the drudgery of these unexciting chores, I met Dr AS in his OPD to get first-hand information about my husband's condition. He told me that MS was improving and they would remove his tubes one by one. This was good news indeed.

Simar went to relieve Reena; she had wanted to buy gifts for her children before going back to Chandigarh but thought it was improper to do so at such a time. That was so old-worldly that I asked Simar to take her to a good mall near the hospital and let her shop to her heart's content.

Mona's father stood in for Paramjit by MS's bedside the next morning. I stayed back because Karan was to come at 1 a.m. for what was initially supposed to be our Orissa trip. He had clubbed it with a conference in Puri, where he was a speaker. He brought loads of diapers for his father. Such were the gifts we appreciated these days. It would take MS a long time (at least a year) to train the bladder fashioned out of a part of the intestines. But the external urinary orifice remained the same and he did not have a hole and a bag in his abdomen to collect the urine. Thank heavens for small mercies. Cancers of the breast or uterus were bad enough but they were organs one could do without; how can one manage without a bladder?

21.3.13

Karan went with his brother to meet his father. I joined them at the hospital after my morning clinic and the three of us went to Haldiram's for lunch. I had dosa, Simar his favourite chhole bhature and the health-conscious Karan opted for idli and dahi bhalle. Back at SSCH I decided to make a last-minute bid to reduce the hospital bill. It had far exceeded the estimate they had given us. I entered the OPD and waited till the high and mighty Dr AS deemed it necessary to notice my presence. I had been told that doctors could volunteer to reduce their fees by 10 per cent. This was the least Dr AS could do for a fellow doctor, I thought, but he refused outright. Blinking back tears of humiliation, I stormed out of the room. I was angry with myself for begging favours from a man who was as emotionless as the robots he worked with.

A colleague had promised to help with the bill as she knew the director of the hospital, but she did not pick up the phone though I called several times. Her excuse later was that we should have asked for a rebate before the bill was made and her contact could do nothing now. My kids were annoyed by my persistence but I met Mr Bhardwaj, head of the accounts department, while they waited outside. Even as he was dismissing me with a 'We'll see what we can do about it ...' Rajan rang up. 'I am in the office trying to reduce the hospital bill; will call you later,' I whispered. He promptly asked me to give the phone to the person in charge. His modus operandi was:

a) Look for a commonality between him and the person whose help we needed.

b) Ask if they needed his help for issues troubling them (for he was a very influential man with the right contacts) in exchange for his help – a pure and simple barter of favours.

Within minutes he learnt that Mr Bhardwaj and he were Brahmins and belonged to the same gotra, whatever that meant. By telling him that he was the head of the All India Brahmin Sabha and after dropping a few names, Rajan managed to decrease the hospital bill by one lakh rupees. That too after a phone call to an utter stranger! My sons' embarrassment turned to amazement; I dared not tell them how this miracle had come about!

Thankfully, MS was tolerating liquids and soft diet fairly well by now. Except for the abdominal drain, his tubes had come out one by one. He would be discharged tomorrow or the day after.

22.3.13

My associate consultant had found a more lucrative job elsewhere and would be leaving me in the lurch at such a crucial time. She had taken over much of the mundane work at the hospital while I had devoted myself to MS and his affairs. I had would not be able to find a replacement at such a short notice; this was just another headache that troubled me. Meanwhile, Karan left for his conference and Paramjit returned from Nainital.

MS experienced severe pain when the abdominal drain was removed and needed IV sedation. He would be discharged the coming morning but the moot point was where to put him at home. Downstairs in the nursing home was practical, with the nurses around, though we may also need a male caretaker. Upstairs, on his own bed, in his own room, he would feel better psychologically, but it would not be safe to have a caretaker, a stranger, in our room after the others had left. Anyway, I put a large mackintosh on his bed and took out all the single sheets I had collected during the estranged period of our marriage. During that time, we had slept on twin beds separated by a table in between. The arrival of my parents for a prolonged visit had forced us to shift to the master bedroom with a double bed, though we had stopped being physically intimate after I had opted for intimacy with Rajan.

MS was to come home with a condom catheter attached to his penis. As Paramjit was buying some, he rang up to ask me slyly which size to buy. I told him to ask his chachu and not me. I was unaware they came in sizes.

By nature, MS was an untidy person. I had spent days thoroughly spring cleaning our room in preparation of MS's homecoming. Infection during the weakened post-operative state would be disastrous. Papers, files, bags and briefcases lay on his side of the bed accumulating dust, for we were not allowed to touch them, but now I had no option but to remove them all. Clothes on pegs behind doors were removed. Those that were needed, chiefly cotton kurta pyjamas, I stacked neatly in his cupboard, to which I had finally gained a key. I changed the curtains and removed extra furniture, so that it was now clean, spacious and well ventilated to welcome the invalid home.

23.3.13

Karan turned thirty-eight years old today. Simar and I wished him happy birthday on the phone, as he was still at the conference in Puri, and went to get MS discharged. Asking Simar to stay by his father's side, I went to settle accounts. To my dismay the billing clerk had received no intimation about the hefty discount. Whatever happened to the rebate Mr Bhardwaj had promised us? I marched up to his room, willing to risk further humiliation, before I made the final payment. I knocked and entered to find him in animated discussion with a number of people and dared not risk a rebuttal in front of so many strangers. Even as I contemplated backing out, he said airily, 'Just pay fifty–sixty thousand more than what you have already deposited.'

'But the billing clerk refuses …'

'Meet Miss So-and-So. I have given her instructions.'

Down the labyrinthine corridors I went to find her. The discount exceeded my wildest expectations: Rajan had managed to save us 1.71 lakh rupees.

A cancer hospital is a study in human nature. Angel and demons coexist, as do heaven and hell. For every callous Dr AS there is a Dr Malvika who generously donated her time and blood. For every indifferent nurse in the ward there is a Sister Catherine, a diminutive Keralite who pronounced a burly Sikh her relative so that he received better treatment. There was that kindly man who allotted us the best of rooms within our limited resources, and last but not the least Mr Bhardwaj, who managed the large, unexpected slash in bills thanks to Rajan, who did not have to do what he did for my husband. I also cannot forget Paramjit's dedication. He left his work and aged mother to spend a tireless twenty-one days at the hospital looking after an uncle, when children barely have time for their own parents. I do not think I or my sons would have done so much for Paramjit's father, who mercifully died in a matter of minutes, five years back. I thanked each and every one personally and blessed them from the bottom of my heart. Neither did I forget to include them in my prayers. Malvika had been trying to conceive and had not been successful so far. When she finally did deliver twins after years of infertility treatment, I was ecstatic for her. It seemed as if my prayers had been answered.

Finally, MS was discharged. We bought the medicines he needed over the next 6 weeks from the 40 per cent discount store, which I saw for the first time. I also saw 'Lazeez', the restaurant where Paramjit would have butter chicken every day (Simar was more into Pizza Hut). MS sat in the car with a condom catheter taped onto his penis for he was totally incontinent. This was connected to a urobag, which could be emptied when full. This was a hygienic way to prevent dribbling and avoid infection, which would definitely occur with long-term catheter use. We reached home at 2.30 p.m., but as MS got down from the car and started walking down the driveway, the tape gave way and the urine began to drip. He had to pinch his organ with his thumb and forefinger till he reached our room and switched over to diapers. He was to wear them for the rest of his life, for he never did learn to train his new intestinal bladder.

Choco, our nine-year-old Lhasa Apso, was overjoyed at seeing his master, though, unlike me, MS wasn't fond of dogs. With a furiously wagging tail he put his little paws on the bed and his head on MS's lap. MS felt nice at being welcomed back thus, but we took Choco away quickly as MS was vulnerable to infection.

By evening MS had changed three diapers and also leaked onto his bed. Overwhelmed with fatigue and helplessness, I lay down, plagued by morbid thoughts. What was to become of him, of us? Just then Ruby and family came over with a cake to celebrate MS's return and cheer us up. And cheer us they did. Her grandson was a beautiful toddler, loving and lovable. It felt so nice to gossip and laugh after such a long time. Poor Choco was locked up as he was given to biting on occasion and they were afraid of him.

24.3.13

I slept at 1.30 a.m. and got up at 6 a.m. to see that MS had wet his bed again. After helping him change, I emerged from my room carrying MS's urine-soaked bed sheets for washing while Mona emerged from hers to warm water for Jessy's milk – both of us were looking after the helpless in our care. She had on her face the happy fatigue of caring for a blossoming life while I had on my face the depressed fatigue of looking after a fading life. Paramjit had stomach ache and loose motions (perhaps too much butter chicken) so I had another person to care for.

The exertion and relentless toil of the preceding days took their toll on Simar too, for he was as prickly as ever. I called the insurance agent and applied for reimbursement while Simar made copies of the relevant papers as the originals had to be deposited with the insurance company. An outstation friend of Mona's came over to look her up and rave over her newborn. Simar took them out leaving the baby in my care. I enjoyed exclusive baby time and watching him gurgle and play and do what babies usually do – sleep, pee, drink milk, play. Such a change from looking after an invalid!

25.3.13

MS was trying to brave it out without troubling anyone but it was difficult. His sister Amrit was keen to visit but I told her that it would be more practical to come during chemotherapy; her help would be more appreciated then.

26.3.13

Overwrought nerves led to a short fuse. Simar and I had another tiff in the morning because the internet was not working again and he thought I had skimped on money and bought a poor connection. Added to the chronic fatigue that threatened to overwhelm and the stress of caring for a cancer patient was the tension of an exacting profession. Though a veteran, with over thirty years in active practice, I could be stumped by certain cases. That night, I had performed a difficult emergency caesarean on a patient with two previous caesareans who had come in labour. The uterus was stuck to the abdominal wall and dense adhesions were making it difficult to gain access. The paediatric resident waited and waited for the baby, which was usually extracted within minutes of opening the abdomen. Her senior thought she was being careless and asked what was taking her so long. She replied, 'The obstetrician cannot find the uterus!' This was unbelievable, for where could such a huge organ with a fully grown baby inside hide, but she was stating a fact. The abdominal wall was plastered to the uterus in such a way that we could not see where one ended and the other began. What if the bladder and intestines were sandwiched between the two and got injured while making the incision? It would be catastrophic. I had no option but to go ahead. With a prayer on my lips, I made the incision. Luckily it was on the uterus but that did not end our woes; the umbilical cord popped out of the incision while the head remained high up, like a ball that I was unable to grasp. In desperation I caught hold of a foot, turned the baby around and brought it out as breech! Its lusty cry was the sweetest sound I had heard in weeks. Cases such as these shorten an obstetrician's life by years!

At home I had this huge sick baby to tend to. He would whine weakly to gain sympathy, but the moment he got a call from a patient and he thought I was out of earshot, he'd talk normally, even loudly at times. This was because he did not want people around his workplace to know that he had cancer, lest it affect his practice. He had it known through his compounder that he was operated for prostate enlargement. Out of the blue Paramjit asked me one day, '*Aise log maze le sakte hain kya* (Can such people enjoy sex)?

'Ask your chacha,' I retorted.

Simar whispered to me, 'Tell him, "at least not with me"', for it was common knowledge that I had stopped sleeping with MS after I got involved with Rajan.

27.3.13

Karan returned from Puri at 2 a.m. He had to give a talk at Le Meridien at 2 p.m. that very day. I would have liked to hear him speak but he did not want me to come. I learnt from friends that it was a resounding success. My heart swelled with pride.

MS's sister Amrit could stay back no longer. She arrived with her husband early in the morning from Bengaluru, got us presents and cried copiously for her dear brother. I too lavished expensive gifts on them as was the custom at the birth of a grandson. This was the first time she would be seeing Jessy. MS's cancer, his surgery and the postoperative complications had come in the way of us enjoying the antics of our beloved grandchild. In fact, some cruelly superstitious people had insinuated that he was unlucky for his grandfather!

Today was Holi, Jessy's first Holi, and his mother decided to celebrate it despite the gloom that prevailed. This changed my brooding mood. She had dressed her two-and-a-half-month-old son in an off-white kurti, koti and dhoti. I applied a black tika on his cheek to ward off evil spirits. The entire family applied a paste of haldi, water and besan on him and soiled his clothes (that was the very idea), ate sweetmeats and danced on the terrace to the beat of music belted out by the blaring DJ in the park across the road, where Holi was being celebrated by the entire colony.

During a lunch of puri-aloo, Karan tried to kick my volatile Choco away and almost got bitten in the process. Nastily, he blamed me for his behaviour. I tried telling him that the poor fellow was unaccustomed to crowds and that one does not kick a Lhasa, for they are temperamental dogs, but he retorted, 'A murderer's mother will never acknowledge the fact that her son is a murderer.' And then he hit me where it hurt most, 'Now don't go and write a poem on this.'

Stung to the quick, I replied, 'I can't promise you that, but rest assured, I will not send it to you.'

I was and am still very sensitive about my writing, though finally a manuscript had been accepted and I was well on my way to becoming a published author. A similar thing happened years later with my Simar.

'Get off that pile of stones immediately,' he scolded his naughty little boy, Jessy.

'It is called rubble,' I blurted. Undermining Simar's authority was definitely not my aim, but he saw it that way. He hit back by calling me 'a bloody thesaurus'. Stung to the core, I retorted, 'Bloody cook,' though he was a chef of no mean acclaim. Mona ticked off Simar saying this was no way to speak to his mother. Later, she asked me, 'Why did he say dinosaurs?' This was much too funny and we laughed till tears ran down our cheeks. At least he did not think I was that old.

Thankfully, Sauruv, our efficient old help, had returned, though he had taken leave for Holi. Amrit and I made some nutritious soup and laid the table, and we ate in gloomy silence, each lost in sombre thoughts. Karan and Simar had gone to Ruby's house for dinner and returned at 11 p.m. Karan was grumpy because he did not want to share his bed with Amrit's husband or Paramjit. He preferred sleeping alone on a folding bed in the drawing room and berated me for not getting it ready. What did he think of himself, God's gift to our clan that I wait hand and foot on him? He could very well do it himself.

As it was that time of the year when one put away winter clothes and took out summer clothing, Amrit sorted out her brother's clothes, while he gave instructions. Whatever his faults, I was spared the chore of taking care of his things, like other wives. This was only because he was possessive about his belongings and would not trust anyone else with them. MS could not part with a single item, old or new. He got frayed collars turned inside out and faded T-shirts dyed. This last was being pennywise and pound foolish, for they bled in the washing machine, destroying the nicer clothes. Not even Amrit could persuade him to dispose of the surplus, old-fashioned clothes. I doubt he would have changed his stance if he knew of the number of clothes I would give to charity after his death.

28.3.13

I did a major laparoscopic surgery early in the morning. Usually, I hurried back soon after my work to be with MS as much as possible, but today I attended an important departmental meet knowing that Amrit was taking care of her brother and training the help to prepare nutritious broths for him. As for my sons, they went for an English movie along with Paramjit. Karan was here for but a few days and if this was the quality time he was spending with his sick father … I wondered. Years ago, he had behaved in a similar manner with his dying grandmother, who had loved him dearly. At that time, he could allay his conscience by saying that her Alzheimer's would prevent her from recognising him anyway. Though I felt bad for MS, he did not seem to mind. In his place, I would have felt forsaken, but MS was essentially a simple man with simple needs, nice enough as long as you did not ask him to spend.

Earlier, they had taken him to Big Bazaar, where he shopped for groceries like in old times. It pleased him very much. Happily tired, he slept. Come to think of it, MS had interacted with his sons only in a basic way during their growing up years and they were never really close to him. On the other hand, I was so much into their affairs that more often than not I offended them; with MS they were non-committal.

Paramjit returned soon after the movie as he had to leave for Nainital that night. I blessed him from the bottom of my heart, for he had been very helpful, just like his deceased father. This meant that nurture triumphed over nature, that is, traits were not necessarily inherited (he was an adopted child though he did not know it), and one tends to emulate what one sees. Maybe Karan and Simar behaved in the way they saw their father behave towards me. Now they were at CP buying books, having dinner – kathi rolls and kebabs at Nizam's. It was just another holiday for Karan.

MS took no interest whatsoever in his disease. He did not ask the doctor a thing, did not look up the net for five-year survival rates or take a call on what he wanted to do with the time he had left. He did not discuss his fears and phobias with me and continued as if nothing was amiss. He also did not give in to bouts of hysteria or depression or express gratitude to those taking care of him. He remained in a state of denial till the very end; maybe that was his coping mechanism. I on the other hand obsessively looked up the net, absorbing all there was to know about his cancer, its progress, prognosis, etc. I learnt that hair dye could contribute to bladder cancer, though it was the older variety no longer in use that contained carcinogens. What I did know was that MS was allergic to hair dye, but his vanity did not allow him to age gracefully. Each time he dyed his greying beard, angry red eruptions would appear on his cheeks. He would apply ointments on the rash but he would not stop using the dye. I also learnt that the five-year survival rate for bladder cancer with lymph node spread was only 15 to 20 per cent, which left me deeply depressed.

I could barely contain my tears when MS did ardaas for Paramjit before he left. Little things such as these was what

I would miss when he was no longer around. I had begun to savour and store in memory his mannerisms to remember him by. The way he would lean back in his chair when the help put another full-blown phulka fresh off the tawa on his plate, the way he would release the hot air out of it by pressing the back of a katori on it, the way he would squeeze the lemon from the salad into his glass of water, put black pepper in his dal as it was an antioxidant … though all the antioxidants in the world could not protect him from cancer and its aftermath.

He took no active interest in the management of his disease, nor did he assert himself. He had abdicated that right when he spent nothing for his own treatment, which left himself at the mercy of my goodwill. I too began to appreciate his resilience and his contribution to our household expenses. Having cribbed about his miserliness all my married life, now that the entire financial burden was on me, I realised that there was quite a bit of expenditure that he bore.

29.3.13

Every day while driving to work, I would pass a silk cotton tree in flower. It was in a school campus and I thought the students in the upper section were lucky to have its large scarlet blossoms smile at them through the windows of their classrooms. Today, I was aghast to see that all its branches had been chopped off. Unaccountably, I began to cry and could not stop. It was as if I had been maimed, for my support systems had been chopped off one by one – Karan had settled abroad, MS was dying and Simar would soon leave for another city. Though, like the tree, I stood tall and erect, I was broken inside. The coagulated sap on its stumps spoke of its pain more eloquently than screams. My soul splintered, my heart bled and my eyes burned, as I drove past.

As MS would need chemotherapy (it usually started six weeks after surgery, when the patient's general condition had improved) in the near future, we decided to meet a reputed oncologist at SSCH beforehand to discuss the issue. We caught him on his rounds just before he entered the medical ICU, introduced ourselves and told him that we needed to consult with him. He asked us to wait outside his OPD room and he would see us shortly. So we paid his fees and waited and waited … I don't know why, but maybe because this place was too busy, the doctors did not think of patients (even if the patient was a doctor) as people who needed attention though we paid dearly for their time. Perhaps they had become desensitised to death and decay and did not care. Disillusioned once again, we decided this was not the place for us and left.

Then began the search for another cancer hospital that was good and nearby; after all, I would have to manage alone henceforth. After much surveying we zeroed in on Asha Cancer Hospital (ACH). Though there were still a few weeks to go, we decided to visit the place while Karan was here to gauge the atmosphere and the competency of the doctor. The hospital was spacious, clean and airy, a vast change from the claustrophobia of SSCH. We met a Dr Verma (who seemed good enough) and discussed the logistics with him. It would cost us thirty to forty thousand rupees per cycle. As we were talking MS started feeling weak and rested on the examination table. There was discomfort in his abdomen with mild distension.

Back home, MS lay down to gather his strength, for he had decided to commence his practice that very evening. We tried to dissuade him but he was adamant. We feared that he would catch an infection at this vulnerable stage but he thought a mask would be protection enough. Reluctantly, we agreed. Maybe this was the incentive he needed to keep going. I could not help but appreciate his willpower and resilience in the face of adversity. I do not think anyone else would have gone to work so soon after such a major surgery, with postoperative complications of such a dreadful disease.

People have cancer-phobia. Some even think it is contagious and would look for other options if they came to know their doctor had cancer. We dropped MS at the clinic with Amrit's husband (so that he could keep an eye on him) and whiled away our time in a movie hall nearby so that we could pick him up later. However, MS's ambitious plans to resume practice were thwarted that very night, for his abdominal discomfort and distension increased. This was followed by spasmodic pain and vomiting that kept us awake the whole night.

30.3.13

As Simar had last-minute business to attend to before leaving for Bengaluru, Karan and I took MS to the emergency at SSCH. We were told that as it was Saturday and Dr AS was in the OPD, it would be quicker to take MS there. The moment Dr AS arrived I followed him inside and began telling him about MS's condition. Even as a junior doctor, who had been my junior before joining SSCH, got up to offer me a chair, true to form, AS pulled an AS on me – his worst so far.

'Don't jump the queue, madam,' he said in front of his entourage and the patients crowding his large room.

'But it is an emergency,' I managed to sputter, wanting to add, 'a complication of your surgery,' but dared not.

As a rule, Karan sided with whoever was against me and this time was no exception, for he said, 'I too hate pushy females in my OPD.' He was a liver specialist in the United States and did have a knack of hurting me.

Thus, unceremoniously thrown out, Karan and I awaited our turn while MS writhed on a trolley in the treatment room. After taking his own sweet time, the doctor examined

MS and told us to admit him in daycare and get an X-ray done. Soon we found ourselves in a dingy little cubicle. Right in front lay an emaciated man with a surgically excavated face undergoing chemo, vomiting occasionally into a bucket by his side while his wife watched TV without a flicker of emotion.

IV fluids were started and I went back as Karan stayed back with his father for the X-ray. Around noon Karan rang up to say there were air-fluid levels and MS needed admission for partial intestinal obstruction (probably due to adhesions). Once again, I opted for an economy room and told Karan to meet the manager who had been helpful earlier. He would give us the best bed available within our budget. We got a room by a large glass window instead of the claustrophobic middle bed he was getting earlier. Karan got a taste of what we all had been through as he had to run around for medicines too.

Amrit and her husband had gone to meet relatives in Delhi and to pray for MS's speedy recovery at Bangla Sahib. Though she made noises about staying back, I told her there were enough of us around to take him to the hospital. When she learnt that he had been readmitted, she reached the hospital to see him. Simar would be staying with his father for the night.

31.3.13

This was one of the few times Karan and I sat down to actually talk, as for once we were both on the same side. We were discussing the financial aspect of MS's treatment and I said, 'I did not know that you would eventually send money, *phir bhi maine pani ki tarah paisa bahaya* (I spent money like water), though I know that had the shoe been on the other foot, he would have done nothing for me.'

'But Papa must be having some money saved.'

'I think a lot went into the purchase of the shop, though I do know that he does not want to break his PPF, which matures in 2014, even for his own treatment.'

'Tell that bastard that he may not be around in 2014 to utilise it!' said Karan, which horrified me.

'You tell him,' I retorted.

Simar rang up to say that he was feeling unwell. I asked Karan to sit by his father tonight.

'Send someone else.'

I could not go as I had to manage a house full of relatives, including the newborn and his post-caesarean mother, and no one else knew the working of my household. I marched to Amrit's room and asked if she could be with MS tonight. She agreed immediately, which showed Karan in a bad light. He tried to backtrack by pretending that he had not said what I thought he had said. Indeed!

All of us were overwrought, overworked and irritable, but Karan took the cake. Did he not have a single kind bone in his body? He had offered blood for his father and sent money (rather late) which I knew he would rub in sooner or later; it turned out to be sooner rather than later. When I told him that Simar and Paramjit often ended up being with MS for twenty-four hours at a stretch, he replied viciously through clenched teeth, 'I sent the money so that I would not have to sit with him.'

If I'd had the money in hand, I would have thrown it on his face.

Amrit and her husband relieved Simar for the rest of the day. Perforce Karan had to do night duty. I took him to the hospital in the evening. While he sat with his father, Amrit and I walked around the campus that Sunday evening and beheld a beautiful sight – a peacock from the adjoining woods had alighted on the hospital driveway. After walking about regally for a while, it took wing, its magnificent tail trailing, and landed in the dense foliage of a tree.

The resident doctor on evening duty was frank about the perils of MS's subacute intestinal obstruction as it had shown no sign of improving. Vociferously, he gave negative inputs right in front of MS, which brought tears to the poor man's eyes. Just as we had begun to despair, MS passed flatus! It was the sweetest sound we had heard in days, the smell notwithstanding. The intestines had broadcasted loud and clear that they were back on duty. MS was now allowed a soft diet and was ravenous. Happily, I watched him gobble up the meagre portion of khichdi served, famished as he was after the cancer-wrought internal famine. In three months, he had given 7 kilos of his flesh to the disease. In my heart arose an infinite pity for this man.

Having devoured the contents of his bowl, he asked for more. So Karan and I went to the nursing counter to ask the nurse to ring up the hospital kitchen for more khichdi. '*Ungel ko phook lagi hai* (Uncle is hungry)?' she asked in her heavily Malayalam-accented Hindi, which had us in splits especially for using the word phook (gas) for bhook (hunger). She was inadvertently right – for the passing phook accounted for his bhook.

As MS slept, we went to Haldiram's to celebrate his fart! Amid the lavish repast, remembering her brother's weakness for good food, Amrit burst into tears. After dinner, we walked Karan back to the hospital and looked up MS before we went home. He was snoring peacefully. When I was taking my leave, Karan kissed me goodbye as if the venom he spewed could be erased by a perfunctory kiss. As we were walking down the corridor towards the lift, my phone rang. I stopped to fish it out of my bag while Karan and his aunt walked ahead lost in earnest conversation. As I caught up with them, I heard him conclude bitterly, 'This is why I cannot bear to stay here more than a week.' Each word was a hole punched into my heart. As Abraham Varghese wrote in his book *Cutting for Stone*, 'No blade can puncture the human heart like the well-chosen words of a spiteful son.'

1.4.13

Karan was cranky after spending just one night at the hospital with people coughing and dying around him. Thankfully, MS was discharged from SSCH. I sincerely hoped that this was the last we would see of a hospital that evoked such horrible memories.

The second admission, soon after a prolonged stay after a major surgery for advanced cancer, took its toll. MS was tired, weak and susceptible to infection. After a light meal he slept for a few hours, only to get up utterly ashamed of himself. He had wet his bed despite the diaper. With the servant's help, I got him clean and dry again. We tried to make him do bladder training exercises but he could not get the hang of it. The only alternative left was to change his diapers frequently. This was not always possible at night and I had to get up more than once to dry him up.

The maid refused to wash his urine-soaked clothes. We would have to buy a washing machine. It's not that we could not afford one earlier, it was just that it was convenient to get our clothes washed by hand and we hadn't felt the need to buy one. Paradoxically, our maid had a washing machine at home, while she washed our clothes manually. We had discussed the issue when cancer was not even a remote possibility but MS would not agree. Every major expense would be shared equally between us, so I would be contributing half, but the washing powder for hand-washed clothes was cheaper than that needed for the machine. Moreover, there was the electricity bill to consider, which was MS's department, so he would not hear of installing one. The circumstances had changed, and thanks to his urinary incontinence, a washing machine had become a necessity now.

Apart from making my will, another important item on my agenda was a family photograph. I did not know when the four of us would be together again but Karan was very sleepy after his night duty by his father's side and Simar had to attend to matters regarding his shifting. So leaving MS to rest I went for my evening OPD. Finally, we got our act together at night and took a lot of pictures of the four of us along with Jessy and Mona. If MS understood the urgency of these photographs, he said nothing.

We had a sumptuous dinner of soup and chicken with spinach, which to our pleasant surprise MS shared with us at the table. Not for him the invalid's tray in bed. That was indeed a positive sign. Just then Simar, at the instigation of his wife, scolded Sauruv for not cleaning their room, adding for good measure, 'What do you get paid for?'

The poor fellow had wanted to clean Mona's room in the morning but she was nursing her baby and had refused him entry. After that he had been slogging in the kitchen and with MS the whole day long and did not find the time to do so. Annoyed, Sauruv wanted to leave immediately. Amrit and I pacified him and begged Simar to be more tolerant, as we were solely dependent on him at this crucial juncture.

Amrit had begun torturing herself for the sake of her brother, in the hope that God would listen to her prayers. She stopped eating sweets and would get up at three every morning to complete the Sukhmani Sahib path. She told me that earlier she had never felt the need to do path routinely and would pray that God give her motivation to do so. Now it was her brother's cancer that was the motivation!

Bhabiji (Paramjit's mother) too experienced the negative aspect of having her wish realised. Every winter the entire clan, that is, my father-in-law, mother-in-law, brother-in-law, his wife (Bhabiji) and son Paramjit, descended from Nainital to our home in Delhi to avoid the bitter cold of the hills. The drudgery of housework fell on Bhabiji in Nainital. Though she did what all housewives did, her standard refrain was, '*Mera ji karda hai ki koi maino hath vich khana de* (I wish someone would serve me food in my hands).'

She longed to relax and be waited upon, and lo and behold, when her bilateral TKR (total knee replacement) surgery did not go as well as expected, she spent six months bedridden being waited upon hand and foot. She got what she had longed for, but all she wanted now was to be up and about. I also remembered a story about a couple who desperately wanted wealth. A fairy appeared and asked them, 'Are you sure you want to be rich at any cost?' Yes, they said in unison, and lo and behold, their only son, a soldier, died at war and they got lakhs in gratuity. This reminded me of the saying, 'Be careful what you wish for, you just might get it.'

2.4.13

Simar took MS to Big Bazaar for a change of scene and a taste of normalcy as MS enjoyed buying groceries. Later, Simar, Karan and Mona went to Khan Market to shop and eat out. Amrit and I enjoyed looking after the baby and bitching about our daughters-in-law, in a mild, humorous sort of way. We laughed after such a long time. Tentatively, I told her to ask her brother to pitch in; it was unfair to put the entire financial burden on others. She gave an evasive answer and I left it at that.

Why can't I grow a thick skin? Why does every little thing hurt so badly? Was it my overwrought state? This time it was Simar's turn to hurt me. They had returned from their outing and I was trying to tell him about my day with Jessy when his phone rang. After he had finished speaking, I began again, at which he cut me short by asking me not to repeat myself. I was amazed at his brusque manner when I had been babysitting his son for nine hours and looking after his bedridden father. Seeing the expression on my face, he pursed his lips, crossed his arms and with a look of exaggerated patience prepared himself to listen. This made me want to cry so badly that murmuring I was exhausted I fled from the room.

Karan left for the airport at 11.30 p.m. This was the first time his father had not gone to pick him up or drop him at the airport. He would come and go in a taxi henceforth. After he left, Amrit told me something I had already overheard at the hospital – Karan could not bear to stay here for more than a week. Why does he bother at all, I thought dully, if he leaves so much pain and hurt feelings behind.

I did not like it when my sons bore a grudge against Choco, an animal, after all, who did not know better. Lhasa Apsos are a vicious breed and no amount of training could rid Choco of his habit of biting, though his assaults were invariably provoked. It usually happened when people inadvertently stepped on his tail when he sat under the table during meals. The men were none the worse after the reflex bite as they wore shoes, but the women, with their fancy slippers or sandals, were not so lucky. I too had been the recipient of such snapping, but I understood that it was a reflex action and Choco could not help himself. He would immediately be contrite, for he would literally burrow into me begging forgiveness. I would let him be miserable for a while but he would not budge till my heart melted and I held him close; all would be right with our world again. Naturally this understanding did not exist between him and the others. They were too angry with him or too scared to accept his apologies. Nor were they receptive to his affectionate overtures, for Choco forgot that he was in their bad books for bad behaviour.

This time Karan had tried to kick him away and almost got bitten. To add insult to injury, Choco did what I dared not, snap at Karan, who usually snapped at me, giving him a taste of his own medicine. I dared not smile at the irony of the situation. A short while later, forgetting Karan's nasty behaviour, the imbecile went up to the unforgiving man, wagging his tail. He put his paws on Karan's leg and looked up at his face with shiny, button-black eyes, longing for an affectionate pat, but Karan was in no mood to relent. 'He has the memory of a goldfish,' he exclaimed, shooing my poor Choco away. Didn't he realise that he was just the same – vicious barbs one minute, kisses soon after.

3.4.13

Simar had not recovered completely from his stomach infection and asked me for some medicine. I gave him a strip from my medicine bag and wondered aloud where I had kept the new strips I had recently bought for Karan, who was prone to suffer from Delhi belly whenever he came from the US. Simar cut short my ramblings with a terse 'I don't want all that irrelevant information'.

This was the final straw, inconsequential in itself, but the dam burst and my anguish poured out. I cried and cried for hours non-stop – for what had happened, what was to happen and the fact that everyone would go away leaving me alone to manage henceforth. I cried at the behaviour of my fire-spitting, acid-dripping sons. They had looked after their father physically and financially but without an iota of compassion or respect and extracted their pound of flesh from me.

No one came to wipe my tears except Amrit. MS had enough on his plate already but then he had never shown any kindness towards me. Simar made one meagre attempt to console me by saying that we could get food from outside, which I refused, so he withdrew into a shell.

Mona's life revolved around her baby; she did not concern herself with anything else. Perhaps she bore her own grudges. Perhaps she felt neglected, robbed of the glory that was due to her for giving us an heir. Finally, she handed the baby to me thinking this would cheer me up. When I was totally spent, I got up to give Jessy a bath. The beauty of his form, the pleasurable physicality of the process did indeed distract me.

MS started going to his evening clinic today with Simar, though he drove himself. I went with Amrit to Rani Bagh to buy things for our respective grandchildren. We came back early, as I was expecting a visitor regarding a book deal. It meant a lot to me but no one in my family cared or helped nurture my passion. Instead, after every unpleasant episode, I was told 'Now don't go and write about this …' It was true that I poured out my pain in words and could never write when happy or content, but what about the wellness books, the book of poems and a joke book? Those did not reveal the disgusting details they so dreaded. So why weren't they read or appreciated?

4.4.13

Today I performed a hysteroscopy D&C on a villager called Khimuli. Her husband humorously calls her Kheera Mooli (cucumber, radish). An ayah at the hospital calls the scanty coffee we get in little paper cups from our hospital canteen, polio drops! Nothing like laughter to soothe frayed nerves and ruffled feathers. Despite the situation at home, I made it a point to continue working, for it took my mind off the sombreness that prevailed.

6.4.13

Performed some mundane but unsatisfying chores (half of which MS used to do earlier). Amrit was leaving today but I was held up at the hospital for a delivery and wasn't at home for the goodbyes. Brother and sister bid a tearful farewell to each other. He was her only living blood relative, as her parents, elder sister and brother had expired over the past decade. She was the only person in the world who loved him selflessly, though I would suffer the most when he was no more. She had family to support her, as she lived with her husband, son and daughter-in-law and had a loving married daughter who visited frequently. I shuddered at the thought of a lonely future bereft of all things familiar.

Amrit had finally persuaded her brother to buy a washing machine, though he did not need much persuasion this time. We bought an expensive one with a high capacity, for he was soaking bed sheet after bed sheet with urine, and the washerwoman was creating a fuss. It arrived in the afternoon but would be installed on Monday. As was our practice, I paid half the price, which, if MS had had any decency, he would not have taken from me.

During the division of expenses, he had allocated to himself the duty of buying medicines for whosoever fell ill in the family. This was because, being a family physician, he bought drugs in bulk and was well acquainted with the wholesale market, where medicines cost the least. He had no qualms about giving me expired medicines which I used to swallow without checking, for how could I even dream that he would do such a thing. Surprisingly, they worked, for I realised that besides losing a percentage of their potency, expired medicines cause no harm. My emotions however did not escape unscathed. It showed how little he cared for me. I developed diabetes three years ago and needed the expensive medicine Galvusmet for management. I also needed emotional succour. All I got from MS was a curt, 'Your medicine bill is beyond me. Buy them yourself from now on.'

Each time I bought my monthly stock of medicines the hurt came back. Now that the tables had turned, and he needed expensive chemotherapy, did he expect me to forgive and forget? I was not taken in by his puppy dog looks any more. It was a weapon he had used effectively in the past.

People say that infidelity is the prime cause of marital discord, little understanding that constant bickering over money also takes a heavy toll. I did not expect him to take care of my personal expenses, I bought my car, petrol, clothes, even my birthday presents myself. I shared the household expenses too, but forcing me to wake up drenched in sweat by putting off the AC to reduce the electricity bill was just not done. I would quake whenever the electricity bill arrived, steeling myself for the unending diatribe.

Long before I 'strayed', MS had made a duplicate key of my cupboard and robbed me of every single paisa. He was deep in debt after being lured into gambling by goons to whom he had lost atrocious amounts. We had reached the nadir of our marriage but had somehow come out of it and stayed married. After the debacle, he had clamped up without a word of thanks, though I had pawned my jewellery to tide over this calamity. Despite the tortures my infidelity must have inflicted on him, he had refused to give me the divorce I desperately wanted. Whatever his reasons then, keeping me imprisoned in this loveless marriage served his purpose, for now I was spending my time, money, energy and sleep on his cancer-ridden body.

7.4.13

Within a month of his surgery, MS was up to his old tricks. We were companionably reading the morning newspaper on our terrace when he said, 'You should buy the Surf for the washing machine.'

'Surf!' I asked incredulously. The expense of a detergent was what weighed on his mind and pocket when matters of life and death loomed large. He had the effrontery to justify his demand by saying, 'I have not been earning for the past one month.'

'You have not been spending anything either,' I retorted. 'You have not uttered a single word of gratitude till now for all that I have done for you. All you think of is how to bleed me some more,' I cried.

As usual, it was the little things that hurt the most. I went to Simar's room. They were busy packing as Simar would leave for Bengaluru and Mona for her parents' home. I bathed and dressed Jessy lovingly one last time and saw them off with a heavy heart. From now on it would just be MS and me with his disease and our incompatibility between us.

My parents knew that there was no match between me and the husband my father had chosen for me. Unwilling to admit that they had made a mistake in choosing one inferior to me in upbringing, qualification and income, they put the blame squarely on my shoulders for not 'adjusting'. I could never look up to, leave alone respect or love, MS, though I did all that was expected as a wife and daughter-in-law as best as I could.

Not that he ever treated my parents well. They had stayed with us for a while after spending years in the UK with my brother. Now that my brother's kids were old enough to manage on their own and our parents were no longer needed there, they had come back to India, but they were too old to live alone in their own home. It was decided that Ruby and I would keep them with us turn by turn. As I was the elder, they gave me the 'respect' of staying with me for a few months, though they were happier in their younger daughter's house. This was because her husband was more welcoming than mine and, being a housewife, she could devote more time to them while I was a busy gynaecologist. Most important, they were reluctant to stay in the house of a man who in the largeness of his heart was 'keeping' their wayward daughter. Mummy pitied him and believed that if I washed the dirt of his feet and drank it, it would not be penance enough for betraying such a good man. She could not understand why I had no sense of shame or gratitude.

Ashamed of my behaviour, they took shit from MS uncomplainingly. Despite his stinginess and indifference towards them, my mother took his side in every petty domestic quarrel we had. So I stopped arguing with MS in her presence. As an orthodox woman, she thought it was not right for the girl's parents to stay with the daughter and forced my father to give MS money for staying in his house. This was ridiculous as they had educated me well and I had a substantial income of my own but MS had no compunction in taking their cash – and switching off the AC in their room too! Which girl would respect a husband who did not respect her parents?

The thought of his behaviour towards my father years later, trivial in itself but heart-rending, still brings bile to my throat. After Mummy's death Daddy stayed with us for a while. He was in the habit of eating a fruit a day to keep constipation at bay. As the banana season was over, MS was asked to buy guavas; he bought some, hard as cricket balls, which the poor old man could not get his teeth into. I was mighty glad when Daddy shifted to Ruby's place.

MS had developed a large incisional hernia, perhaps due to the abdominal distension with paralytic ileus soon after his surgery, which made the stitches under his abdominal wall give way. If one did not look above the neck, the pallor, wasted limbs and bulging abdomen made him look like an underweight, anaemic, pregnant woman one saw in government hospitals. The world had become a very sad place to live in indeed.

8.4.13
We finally got a driver called Jagdish for MS today. Once MS started going to work, I could almost believe that everything was normal and even fought with him over our usual sore point – money. Then remembering the bleak future of stage four bladder cancer, I decided to behave kindly towards him.

9.4.13
With death lurking on the horizon, I began sorting out my papers, subconsciously preparing for my demise. Increasingly I thought that with my strong family history, comorbidities and the severe stress I was being subjected to on a regular basis, I could fall dead any time. My grandparents died of heart attack in their sixties. My parents, first cousins who had married for love, gained an extra 15–20 years after bypass surgery. Most of their siblings had stents inserted in their hearts by a cousin, a leading cardiologist in a government hospital in Delhi. When corporate hospitals came up in a big way, offering fat remunerations, he took premature retirement and joined one in Chandigarh. As he was leaving, I said, 'Now that our generation has reached the stage of needing stents, you are leaving Delhi.'

His reply changed my very perspective.

'*Saaf suthri bimaari hai yeh, aaj hain kal nahin* (It is a clean-cut disease – you are here one day and gone the next day).' How very true, unlike cancer, where the 'dying even more than death defines the illness'.

On the other hand, MS remained in a state of denial; it was as if by refusing to acknowledge the disease, it would cease to exist. He would talk of buying a new car and renovating the clinic (he had money for that, apparently).

10.4.13

Though there had been an intensely unhappy phase in our lives, we forgave each other's trespasses and mended our life together. Neither of us raked up past misdemeanours in present quarrels. Peace prevailed in our household as we demanded little of each other. Acute aversions became chronic vexations that we had learnt to live with, as most couples who have lived long enough with each other do. The cessation of expectations led to the cessation of quarrels. Our exacting profession ate up most of our time. The rest of the time, we did our own thing, in companionable silence. He took a morning walk, read the newspaper and watched TV, while I swam or danced, read and wrote books. The other major aspects of married life – cuddles and communication, love and sex – were never there and therefore not missed. Envious of the calm acquired at such a price, the gods would not let us be. Cancer struck, churning the tranquil waters of matrimony into a murky cesspool from which we were attempting to surface and survive.

My heart contracted with pity seeing MS so thin and weak. The skin hung loose on his arms with barely any flesh to support it. His face was scrunched up like a squeezed lemon and his full lips reduced to thin lines. Cancer created a famine within, and despite a nutritious diet, he looked as if he was starving. I prayed that he would not suffer the intense pain cancer patients usually have towards the end. In a rare show of affection, I held his hand and kissed it. No matter what happened, I would stand by him till the end, do whatever was in my power for his well-being, I repeated to myself.

I was so fond of dressing up – putting flowers in my hair, payal on my ankles, wearing toe rings, colourful glass bangles and bright colours that suited my fair skin. All this would stop if I were widowed ... All said and done, there was a lot to be said for having MS around.

Rinku, our former sweeper, came in the afternoon, ostensibly to look up MS but chiefly to see if he could come back. He and Sauruv (who had perhaps asked him to try his luck) had become good friends during their time here together. They thought I would hire Rinku again because of our changed circumstances. He was a good worker and I knew he would wash MS's urine-drenched bed sheets and take good care of him without grumbling like Rani as long as he was paid well, but how could I forget the scandal associated with him.

Perhaps it was because MS and I went to work early, leaving the staff to their own devices, that they behaved with total abandon. When a corporate hospital opened in our locality, I took to doing most of my obstetrical and surgical cases there as my wealthy patients preferred it to the small nursing home I was running. With no work and no supervision, the nurses and the household staff misused our place and resources. Besides raiding my larder, they formed alliances. The nurses pocketed the money they collected for taking blood pressure, giving injections or dressing wounds. Leaving the clinic at the mercy of God, they even went for home visits, giving enemas or inserting a catheter after appropriating the consumables from my stock, and made a tidy sum on the sly. A nurse had taken to selling sealed bottles of antiseptics like Dettol and Betadine to a chemist at half the rate. I caught on when she became bolder and began appropriating bottles of IV fluids.

One may ask that if I had a nursing home of my own, what prompted me to practise elsewhere. Corporate hospitals had come up in a big way with swanky decor and a polite new way of fleecing patients that attracted the rich in droves; the middle class had insurance companies to finance hospitalisation. For the poor, two big government hospitals had come up in the vicinity. MTPs, the bread and butter of gynaecologists, too decreased drastically with the availability of pills that did the work almost as efficiently as a surgical procedure. All this made a serious dent in my practice and left me with free time.

MS cared only for his clinic, twelve kilometres away, and was of no help in running the place. One son was a chef and the other a doctor settled abroad. How long could I slog on alone, especially when stringent new rules pertaining to private medical establishments cropped up every day. It was no longer a cost-effective enterprise. Big fish were slowly gobbling up the little fish, so going by the dictum if you can't beat them, join them, I had joined a corporate hospital. Thus, for a major part of the day, petty thieves with raging hormones had a run of my premises.

I was once perplexed at seeing a broken wooden bench in the rooms reserved for the underprivileged. Much later, after they had sought jobs elsewhere, I learnt from the remaining staff that it broke because a nurse allowed a servant to hump her vigorously on it in lieu of his entire month's salary. Another nurse almost downed a bottle of formalin on learning that her lesbian partner was bisexual. Yet another nurse was addicted to sedatives and almost finished my stock. Away from restrictive families, the restraints of their culture and society, many young nurses tasted a freedom hitherto unknown, which they often misused. I also had the good fortune of having efficient nurses who stayed with me for twelve–fourteen years in the heyday of my nursing home and I will never forget their compassion and loyalty.

In the recent past, a nurse ended up having a torrid affair with the handsome Rinku. That she was engaged to a boy she loved back in Kerala and he had a wife and three children didn't stop them. Rinku squandered his pay on her in return for physical favours, which understandably did not go down well with his wife. She turned up one day and beat the nurse mercilessly with a broom. At this, the nurse cut her wrist with a surgical blade, though not badly enough to sever an artery. I had had enough of their antics and threw them both out. The repercussions of a suicide in my premises were too horrifying to contemplate. Little did I know that the new entrant in our retinue, Jagdish the driver, would add another chapter to such sordid stories and, years later, there would take place in these very premises a successful suicide.

11.4.13

Though Rajan did not intrude in my life, he was unfinished business. Out of the blue he rang up one day to ask for two lakh rupees as his driver needed it to clinch a property deal that very day.

'How can you?' I asked in amazement. 'Instead of offering monetary help to me when I need it, you ask for money, that too for the driver!'

He banged the phone down, but who cared. I had enough on my plate already to cater to the tantrums of an ex-lover. I learnt from Ruby that Rajan had initially asked MH for the same. Though MH's initial response was a no, he decided to lend Rajan half the amount lest he antagonise him. Both parties mistrusted each other but I was not going to intervene.

Rajan had contacts and clout. The police, the judiciary, perhaps the underworld too were in his pocket. He was on back-slapping terms with politicians of both the ruling and the opposition parties and was unanimously selected as the president of the Brahmin Samaj of his area.

This barely lettered man had a standing in society on the basis of which he pursued a flourishing business trading in favours. This had impressed me too in the initial years, for he had been more of a help to me than my husband ever was in carrying out a man's job. I remain indebted to him on that score.

In the heyday of our alliance, I was taken in by the pretence that he helped my people so that they would appreciate his worth and agree to our relationship. I would pity him, for I knew that they were just using him and he could never become a part of the family. Now that I was no longer enamoured by him, I caught on to his game. Quite like Heathcliff in *Wuthering Heights*, he let the sore they had inflicted on his ego fester for years. Now it was revenge, sweet, secret revenge that he sought. He took sadistic pleasure in making them grovel.

His modus operandi was to play the cat-and-mouse game. After lavishing time, effort and money on them, after a deluge of gifts and lofty promises, he would suddenly become unavailable. This led to frantic phone calls by those desperate for his help. The power he wielded over them was a salve to his wounded vanity. Only after he felt that he had punished them enough (without their knowledge) would he deign to help those who hated his guts for ensnaring me. Nothing could give him a greater kick than that.

MH had sought the help of my 'patient' years ago, when he put the registered name of a well-known company on his new showroom. He would have had to pay lakhs in damage had not Rajan's negotiating skills got the matter settled out of court. Having witnessed Rajan's prowess in making the impossible possible, MH had asked Daddy to seek Rajan's help in *his* tangled property matters, the most dangerous of which was to get villainous land grabbers off his land, and Rajan had managed to do so. How could Daddy, who had once threatened to kill him with his licensed revolver, take his help, I wondered.

Rajan had the irritating habit of giving me a detailed account of his interactions with my family. What would be the use of doing my family a favour without making me beholden to him, but these days I had serious issues of my own to tackle. I did not have the time for prolonged telephone conversations regarding matters of no concern to me but he would go on and on. This put me on edge, for I had categorically told him that he was not doing me a favour. He could refuse for all I cared, but he was not one to let go of this golden opportunity for personal vendetta.

He elaborated on the welcome he received in the very house from which he was once barred entry. Rajan had begun to think of Daddy as a father figure, for they had forged a deep bond fighting Daddy's battles together. As 'payment' all that Rajan wanted from my father, a very senior retired official, was a recommendation letter, which Rajan still counts among his most treasured possessions.

Mummy had expired and Daddy was living with MH and Ruby before he left for the UK to join our brother. He was old and ailing and we all knew that we would never see him again. Rajan knew this too and longed to meet Daddy one last time before he left but was not allowed to do so lest he tarnish my sister's reputation too. Soon after, Daddy died on foreign soil.

Coming back to the present, the more Rajan got entrenched in the affairs of Ruby's husband, the more he was enjoying himself. He even offered to lend them capital to buy the entire place from the 'new owners' of the upper floor! Full of his own magnanimity, he told me on the phone, '*Jab kisi ki madad karo to puri tarah se karo nahin to mat karo* (If you help someone do so wholeheartedly or don't help at all).'

'What about me? *Pahaad jaysi musibat jo mere ooper toot padi hai, uska kya* (What about the mountain of troubles that has befallen me)?'

'You are strong,' he said nonchalantly. I banged down the phone.

If I did not know better, I would have been jealous of his attention to my sister but bringing those who had spurned him down on their knees was his life's ambition. The best part was that they did not even know that it was revenge he was seeking and getting in full measure.

There was no such kick to be got for helping me now when there was a decided cooling of ardour on my part, despite his prowess in that department. Maybe failing hormones with advancing age had something to do with it. Poor is an attachment glued merely by physical desire. It has to fall apart when the froth of passion subsides, for there is nothing left to bind it. These days, I could not forgive his faults (worst were his bragging and lying), as I had done in the past, when I was blinded by the pleasures of the flesh he had introduced me to. Now they piled up like driftwood on the shores of a relationship gone dry.

In retrospect, I cannot thank MS enough for not giving me a divorce. After passions plateau, a married couple has the duties of a householder, a social circle, children and relatives to bind them together. With Rajan, I would have been ruined. An outcast, bereft of my children and any kind of social support, totally at the mercy of his diabolic mind, I would have sunk to abysmal depths of misery. A mental wreck, with no place to go to, no person to turn to, the only recourse left to me would have been suicide or the mental asylum.

13.4.13

Today was Jessy's first Baisakhi and the entire clan rang up to congratulate us. There were no elaborate celebrations on account of MS's illness but we went to seek blessings at the local gurdwara. On reaching it, I realised with a shock that the uthala (prayer meeting) of an old lady was going on. As it is, people had hinted that the grandchild was bhari on his grandfather for MS's cancer was diagnosed soon after Jessy's birth. I quickly shook the thought from my mind. After all, one must accept birth and death as part of our existence. They were but the two ends of life, quite like the covers of a book.

We met the head granthi, who was seated on the Guru Granth Sahib dais. He blessed our little boy with amrit (holy water) and put a marigold garland around his neck. I gave him five hundred rupees and told him that after taking his advice we were blessed with a grandchild. Medical treatments including IVF had proved futile. Mona's mother had suggested that the couple should bathe in a river, discard the clothes they wore and feed a pandit. Instead of the flowing waters of a river (the Yamuna was too dirty to take a dip in), they bathed in the sarovar at Bangla Sahib Gurdwara, and instead of a pandit, I had called this Sikh granthi home for a meal, turning the ritual into a fine blend of her religion and ours. All this happened during shrad, an inauspicious time of the year when Hindus pray for the souls of the departed and feed Brahmin priests. As the granthi was eating he asked me whose shrad I was performing. I told him that I was feeding a holy man at the suggestion of my daughter-in-law's mother as she was trying for a child. At this he said, '*Tussi Sikh ho ke vi eh gall nu mande ho* (Despite being a Sikh you believe in such things)?' He suggested that we go to Baba Budha Sahib, as the saint had granted a son to our fifth Guru. Though we continued with infertility specialists, we went there to pray for a child and promised to come back for thanksgiving once we were blessed with a baby. Sure enough, this time the IVF cycle succeeded and nine months later Jessy came into our lives after an eight-year wait. I recollected all this as we sat in the gurdwara with Jessy in my arms and hugged him tight.

Despite myself I could not help but compare the budding of one life and the withering of another. Across the aisle in the men's section of the gurdwara sat MS looking wan and weak. He had stopped colouring his beard and the exposed white roots made him look years older. Was it coincidence that even as the seed of life was sown in Mona's womb the seed of death was sown in MS's body? Both took root and grew to fulfil their destiny. There were no negative feelings towards my beloved grandchild, for he had brought along with him a sense of immortality. A part of all of us would live on in him after we were dead and gone.

Thankfully, MS's willpower was still intact; he went to his clinic every evening without fail. Jagdish drove him to and fro and at my insistence kept an eye on MS during this time in his vulnerable state. Paradoxically, while I discouraged visitors at home to prevent infection, MS was exposed to the sick every day at the clinic. Foolishly, he thought that a mere mask would protect him. I gave in reluctantly for keeping his spirits up was as important as nurturing his physical health. Patients with flu, fever, colds, diarrhoea and dysentery and dengue flocked in his clinic during the 'season'. If he caught some life-threatening infection in his debilitated state, so be it. If he chose to go down doing what made him happy instead of trying to prolong by a few more months, a measly existence in an extremely dissatisfied state of mind, who was I to stop him?

Truth is stranger than fiction. Was the place cursed? Till the five who earned their living in these premises were tenants, their businesses flourished. As soon as they bought these shops, they began falling like ninepins. Hardly any survived long enough to savour their hard-earned gains. Uncannily, calamity after calamity befell all five in quick succession. The one with the corner shop died of a massive heart attack. MS's shop was second in the row, and he had developed cancer that would take him sooner or later. The photographer on his right had a stroke. His son took over the business and, after a major family dispute, took his own life in that very shop. The next belonged to a jeweller who lost a lengthy legal battle and was now heavily in debt. The tailor at the far end cut his losses and sold his shop before some misfortune befell him. This brought to my mind my uncle in Kamla Nagar, who died of a massive heart attack in his chemist shop at the age of thirty-five, leaving behind a thirty-one-year-old widow with three children. A surgeon bought the shop and ran his clinic there for a few years only to die exactly at the age of thirty-five, leaving behind a wife and five kids.

Sauruv had become indispensable, and what's more, he knew it. To exploit the situation, he asked us to allow him to bring his family from the village so that they could live with him. We agreed knowing full well what a drain it would be on our resources. Besides the free lodging, electricity and water, there would be pilferage of food. Even now he ate more than both of us and our dog put together, but as he was an efficient worker and such employees were difficult to come by, we had no choice but to consider it collateral damage.

Sauruv had brought his wife, Kamla, to our house some years ago, as a newlywed, newly pregnant gauche village girl. She took a lively interest in matters and gadgets that the city-bred took for granted. She also managed to create havoc in people's relationships. Till now, I had maintained a cordial relationship with my in-laws. Bhabiji, who lived in Nainital, was recuperating in our house in Delhi after bilateral knee replacement surgery. Though she was knitting sweaters for Kamla's unborn baby and I would be delivering her free at my nursing home, she had no compunction in carrying tales to and fro. Thankfully, we caught on to her game soon enough and made peace with each other. As for getting her delivered by me, the couple feared that I would perform a caesarean section on her. Why on earth would I do that? I had nothing to gain from them financially, even if I were a mercenary kind of doctor. Finally, she had a very difficult vaginal delivery at the primary health centre, where the nurse left a swab in her vagina while stitching her up. The first they learnt of it was when she began to emanate an awful smell and passed copious amounts of greenish-yellow pus from her vagina. She could barely manage to get up. Her in-laws took her newborn daughter and abandoned her. Even as they waited for her to die, her father-in-law found a new bride for his 'soon to be widowed' son and Sauruv willingly went with him to see the girl. Thankfully, a neighbour forced them to take Kamla to the hospital, where the offending object was removed and, after a course of intravenous antibiotics, she was as good as new. She never forgave her in-laws for abandoning her at the crucial time especially as she was an orphan. Her brother and his wife had got rid of her as quickly as they could by marrying her off to an illiterate, while she was matric pass.

The next time she was pregnant, understandably, she refused to go to a hospital. An untrained midwife made her push before the cervix was fully dilated, which led to prolapse of her internal organs. Unperturbed, the wise old lady asked for *kachhi mahua ki sharab* (the first press alcohol made of mahua flowers). Into this she dipped some cotton with which she pushed the prolapsed genitalia inside, and lo and behold, it stayed put. This intrigued me, for as an obstetrician, I would have had no alternative left but to perform a surgery on her at a later date.

So Kamla came along with her children, kept a clean house and looked after her family well. She would come upstairs off and on and we would talk. Fiction is not conjured from thin air, but is woven like a pearl around a grain of truth. The writer in me was intrigued by her story, which she elaborated in great detail. Though her parents had never seen each other before marriage, though they were mismatched physically, her mother tall and fair, her father short and dark, and wore Mahatma Gandhi–like spectacles, there developed between the two a deep attachment that remained till the very end.

Trouble began when her father brought his sister and her two sons to live with them, soon after she was widowed, and looked after them as his own. The years went by, the sister passed away and her grown-up sons repaid their uncle's kindness by staking a claim on his land. This was unacceptable as, after five daughters, he had a son of his own, who was the rightful heir. At that time, the boy was but a child of eight, while Kamla, being the youngest, was six years old. The upstarts threatened to burn their fields and take away their cattle, if he did not transfer his property in their name. To safeguard his precious pair of oxen, her father slept with his son in the courtyard. That fateful night, the father was ill and her mother exchanged places with him. Kamla quarrelled with her much-pampered brother over who would sleep with their mother and won. Gloating over her rare victory, she clung to her mother like a little monkey and slept under a moonless sky. Their enemies chose that very night to commit a horrendous crime.

Kamla woke to the sound of a thud and something hot and sticky splashed on her face. The men had hit her mother on the head with an iron rod, split open her skull, spattering her blood over the frightened child. They shone their flashlight to locate the son and kill him too. Frustrated at having got mother and daughter instead of father and son, they lifted the sari of the dying woman and thrust the rod up her private parts. What sort of a diabolic mind could violate a woman so in front of her little daughter still clinging desperately to her mother's lifeless form?

Her father lost his mind after the incident. Fearing for his only son, he ran into the jungle carrying the boy on his shoulders, leaving the little girl to fend for herself. He darted wildly hither and thither in the dense keekar forest and stopped only when a thorn pierced his son's right eye! He returned to dig out the silver buried under the mud floor of their hut and went from doctor to hospital till his son's eyesight was restored. Meanwhile a married sister looked after Kamla, the fields and cattle but she had a household of her own to take care of. As a result, Kamla had to take over the responsibilities of the lady of the house while still very young. It was a strenuous life but at least she had independence and monopoly. In due course her brother got married. Soon after, her father fell ill and died.

Kamla was now at the mercy of her brother, who was much too afraid of his wife to take her side. Kamla worked like an unpaid maid in their house. She fed and watered the cattle and worked as a farmhand in their field, killed snakes without compunction, was bitten by bees, but took it all in her stride. Besides cooking and washing, Kamla fetched water from a distant well. What hurt was that, soon after Kamla got married, her brother had a tap fitted in their courtyard so that his wife did not have to perform this strenuous chore. The only joy in her life was the dhol (drum) and majeera (cymbals) that her mother had left behind. During festivals at the local temple, Kamla would sing, dance and play these instruments with abandon.

To get rid of the burden of an unmarried sister, her brother got her married into the first family that would take her without a dowry. He did not care that Kamla had studied till class 10 and that the prospective groom was uneducated. Her would-be father-in-law had seen her working in the fields and thought that such a strong and industrious girl would be a boon to their family. Sauruv was a handsome enough fellow, flush with the money he earned shuttering roofs in Mumbai, and dressed well. No one could tell from his demeanour that he could not read and write.

Kamla was attractive with thick lips and broad nose, though not as good-looking as her husband. Hours of working in the fields had darkened her complexion. The fair and handsome Sauruv, who first set eyes on her on their wedding night, took an instant dislike to her and asked his parents to send her back. As her labours shifted from the fields to the kitchen (Sauruv had a large family – eleven brothers and five sisters besides his parents – she had to cook for the entire clan) her tan disappeared to reveal a fairer skin and Sauruv became quite fond of his industrious wife. Her mother-in-law was a tall, beautiful woman with a sharp tongue and hair so long that she had to stand on the bed to comb it. Her father-in-law doted on her. Like a queen bee, her only function was to appease him in bed and deliver kids. The elder offspring raised the younger ones. One by one they were sent off to the city to earn for the family as soon as they were old enough to do so.

During her pregnancy, I watched Sauruv bring whatever she craved for, be it guavas or the costly off-season mangoes. He even got her an expensive sari for Karva Chauth, the stringent fast without food and water, that wives keep for the health and longevity of their husbands.

Against much opposition from Sauruv and much support from me (as the prospect of educating a girl child was close to my heart), Kamla got her daughter enrolled in a government school. Besides thinking that educating a girl was a waste of time, Sauruv thought this would give his wife an opportunity to form an extramarital alliance when she took her children to school and interacted with the teachers and other parents. Suspicious by nature, he would scold her if she came home late. The initial sheen had worn off and they quarrelled about his drinking and her desire to work. He even took to beating her until I told him that such behaviour would not be tolerated in my house.

I did not have to look far for stories. I got them from my employees, my patients who would spill their angst without reservations, if handled with compassion. My manuscript had been accepted by a leading publisher, and I was on cloud nine as far as my literary career was concerned. At the editor's request I was pruning my manuscript and enjoyed the process thoroughly. In fact, this was the only silver lining to the clouds that hung low over our household.

I am not much into ritualistic religion but went for a kirtan at Sujan Singh Sahib Gurdwara, as Mamaji's request was a command. Moreover, I was indebted to him for visiting MS so often and speaking to the doctors at SSCH on our behalf. As expected, the long, didactic session at the gurdwara induced somnolence. Mamaji had called eminent writers/speakers and gifted them pens. He gave me one too but with one condition: 'Write about the Gurus'. To this, Ruby, ever the conformist, added, 'Write only about good things.'

'You'll have to open a publishing house for me then,' I retorted.

19.4.13

A colleague marvelled at the way I was handling my husband's cancer. Her brother-in-law was in hospital for gallbladder cancer and his wife had gone to pieces. 'It is nice to see you so cheerful though I understand how traumatised you must be inside,' she said.

My response to stress has always been to joke about it, even in the operation theatre, so I said, 'I intend to bring him to our IVF centre's inauguration party on Sunday – *halaal se pehle bakre ko mota karna chahiye* (fatten the goat before slaughter),' I said referring to his chemotherapy that would begin on Wednesday. The chemo might lead to oral ulcers and loss of appetite; I might as well let him enjoy a feast before that.

'Where did you get him operated?' she asked.

'At SSCH by Dr AS.'

'AS! The fraud who rules the roost there!'

'Yes.'

He had tried to operate on her thirty-five-year-old brother for 'bladder cancer' but would not allow her husband, who was a surgeon, in the OT. So they got him discharged and took him to another hospital, where they learnt that he did not have cancer!

'No wonder their five-year survival rates are so good,' she added, which meant the rumours I had heard were true. There did exist a cruel caucus between pathologist and surgeons, leading to unnecessary operations on non-cancerous patients.

For a fleeting moment, I wished the doctor had cheated us too and that MS was cancer-free. I rang up Malvika to reconfirm that MS's lymph nodes were really positive. If not, the staging of his cancer would decrease and his five-year survival chances would increase. She reassured me that the departmental head had checked them in front of her and they were indeed positive.

20.4.13

We went to SSCH for a follow-up with Dr AS though I could barely endure the sight of him. MS wanted to take a peg or two at the party but AS strictly forbade him from taking alcohol before chemo. He also asked for a urine culture report and advised to go for chemotherapy only if it was sterile. I rang up Amrit to tell her about the latest developments as she wanted to be with her brother for his first chemotherapy session. 'Whether his urine is sterile or not, I am coming on Tuesday as my ticket is already booked,' she said. I did need moral support, for God knows what the second phase of cancer management had in store for us.

21.4.13

In the evening we went to a banquet hall for the party thrown by the hospital I worked in to announce the inauguration of our IVF centre. I wore a red georgette sari with a fine gold border and fine polki jewellery to flaunt the colours of a married woman before they faded into the whites and greys of widowhood. Everybody thought I looked stunning and I basked in compliments like 'The life of the party has arrived'.

Everyone asked after MS, not expecting him to be here, and I would say, 'See for yourself.'

This was MS's first outing after his surgery and the poor man carried his diaper along to change in between. It was also his last outing before chemo and I wanted him to make the most of it. I was introduced to the new COO of our hospital and thinking that MS was following me I said, 'This is my husband,' expecting him to come forward. I received a hug for my faux paus from Dr Vinay, who was standing behind me instead of MS! 'I would be more than happy to oblige, if the law allowed it,' he said graciously.

As usual MS was lost to me the moment we entered the party hall. He would make a beeline for the bar but as hard drinks were forbidden before chemotherapy, he had headed for the snacks.

Trying not to feel hurt, I let my wit sparkle and basked in the laughter it evoked. It was as if I had unlocked the gates of my imprisoned mirth after ages and wanted to make the most of it before it was caged again.

PART II

CHEMOTHERAPY

'Cancer is a marathon – you can't look at the finish line. You take it moment by moment, sometimes breath by breath, other times step by step.'

Sarah Betz Bucciero

23.4.13

No one knew what the morrow held for us. MS's first chemo was to be started. He was tense and irritable, and I was terrified of the possibility of side effects. I wanted to buy a bucket with a lid to contain his vomit just in case, but MS did not allow me to do so. Perhaps he thought we were inviting trouble by preparing for it. Personally, I only had Mamiji's cancer to go by. She had been the only patient with cancer in our family (not a blood relative at that), till MS decided to carry forward the banner. Though she had expired years ago, I remembered the uncontrollable emesis and the painful oral ulcers that prevented intake of food and needed IV alimentation. Though these were the cause of sheer agony, the 'milder' side effects like the loss of hair and body mass had a more profound impact. I saw her a few days before her death, a bald skeleton, clad in loose hanging skin, sitting with an IV stand by her and a needle in her vein, begging me to kill her. That this formidable, hefty six-footer whom no one dared cross could be reduced to such a state left me in tears. With misplaced kindness, her husband thought it was his duty as a doctor to prolong her agony. Thankfully, she died of a massive blood vomit a few days later. I never forgot her appearance nor her piteous entreaty, which made me vow never to subject MS to such agony if such a situation arose. I was not aware that oncology had progressed rapidly since then and strong drugs were available to prevent undesirable side effects.

Surprisingly, even at this stage, MS was more preoccupied with the expense than with the disease. Amrit had arrived from Bengaluru to be with her brother and foolishly I poured my angst in her ears. Her sympathies lay with her brother and she wondered how I could be bothered about who spent what when his very life was at stake. I told her that MS neither asked how much was spent on his surgery nor contributed a paisa. I had submitted the relevant papers and applied for medical insurance (to which we contributed jointly). Though it was less than half of what we had spent, it would come handy for the chemo. As the money took a long time in coming, I chastised the LIC agent, only to learn that it had already been put in MS's account some time back. 'But he never told me about it!' I exclaimed. Unaware of the financial dynamics of our family the agent said, 'What difference does it make? May God never give such a disease to anyone,' which showed me in a bad light as a mercenary wife.

That night the wily fellow again tried to gain Amrit's sympathy with that 'poor thing' look of his. The appeal to her sensibilities was not for his cancer or his fear of chemo, which was understandable, but for the expense he was being forced to bear. Thankfully, she did not appeal to my finer sensibilities, for I would have asked her to pay. Sensing that antagonising me would not benefit her brother in the long run, she said, 'It is for expenses such as these that we save money.'

24.4.13

On D-day, he did not want me to go for a swim, as we would get 'late'. Late for what? It wasn't as if he was going to his clinic soon after, but hurrying me unnecessarily was another of his annoying traits. He was responsible for our delay in attending every function throughout my married life because he came home late from his clinic. The moment he returned, however late, I could not take a moment extra for something as basic as using the loo and a quarrel would ensue. I would get into the car in a bad mood and the battle for the car AC would begin. He preferred keeping the windows open to save petrol and let the car fill with polluting puffs of carcinogenic fumes from a revving truck at a traffic signal. When every hair in my body was bristling with bad temper he would say, 'You are looking nice,' at which I would feel like banging my purse on his head!

I had promised myself that I would look after him to the best of my ability but that did not include giving in to unreasonable demands. Finally, Amrit (who would not forgo her yoga sessions for anything) intervened, saying, 'Don't grudge her this hour of exercise. After all, she has to remain fit to look after you.'

I had purposely chosen a Wednesday as I did not have morning OPD at the hospital and would not have to apply for leave for each chemo session. After ardaas in front of Guru Nanak Devji's picture, we left for ACH in MS's chauffeur-driven car for his first chemo. I was grateful for Amrit's presence. There was much delay in starting it as we did not know the protocol. Though we reached early we waited in front of Dr Verma's office instead of making an OPD slip of five hundred rupees (we thought MS would be admitted directly). By this time there was a long line in front of the counter, and finally when we got the slip made, the doctor had left for his morning rounds. So the next time on, we made sure that our file was placed on top of the pile and our turn came early. Dr Verma explained that they had scheduled two chemo agents on day one and a single chemo on day seven. There were to be six such cycles repeated every two weeks.

Finally, MS was admitted to a spotlessly clean daycare room at 12 noon. I was made to sign a document stating that I was aware of the complications of chemo and gave my consent for the same. Did I have a choice? While we waited for the blood reports, properly protected technicians mixed dangerous drugs in a glass-walled mixing room in the ward. MS got lunch from the hospital while Amrit ate what we had brought from home in the waiting area. After premedication with strong antiemetics, chemo started at 4 p.m. and finished at 6.30 p.m., after which the IV line was flushed with 100 ml of saline. Thankfully, there was no retching and vomiting that I had so dreaded. In fact, no patient undergoing chemo, including a child with leukaemia, vomited. We got MS's diaper changed twice. As we had brought along a third, we decided to change the last before going home. They had changed only his pants for pyjamas at the hospital, and to our horror we saw, when he sat up, a patch of urine that had spread to his upper back wetting his vest and shirt. As we had not anticipated such a situation, we had not brought along any change of clothes. So we cleaned him up like a baby, washed the shirt and dried it as best we could under the fan. As I was late for my evening OPD, they dropped me at the hospital and went home. For all our fears, MS tolerated his first chemo well, thank God for that.

One chemo was over, eleven left. 'Let's keep our fingers crossed,' I told Amrit.

From now on MS would be paying for his treatment, which was approximately fifty thousand rupees per cycle. MS clung to his money till the last moment and then gave it in instalments, parting with the initial advance of five thousand rupees first. Foolishly, he kept the rest in his pants pocket, the very pants he kept in an unlocked bedside locker while he changed into hospital pyjamas. He'd rather the ward boy steal it while curtained off for a change of diaper than hand it over to me. Did he think I would appropriate the money when the hospital gave receipts for every rupee it took? It was humiliating and I had to tell his sister what her precious brother was up to. At her insistence he grudgingly began to handing me the entire amount at the outset.

25.4.13

As we were again entitled to an insurance claim during the next financial year, I sent the relevant papers to the LIC agent. MS's cousin rang up to enquire about his health. We knew that her younger sister had recently succumbed to complications of dengue. What we did not know was that she had been treated for stage three breast cancer seven years back. Bone metastasis in the vertebra was diagnosed when she developed severe sciatic pain. Against her better judgement, quite like MS, she attended her busy paediatric OPD while on chemo thinking that a normal blood count would protect her, but she lost her life to an opportunistic infection as the immunity of a cancer person, not very good to begin with, was severely compromised with chemo. The only consolation was that she died doing what she loved, instead of living for a few more painfully unhappy years.

28.4.13

I took in a pigeon with an injured wing, washed and anointed its wounds and kept it safe from predators in a room with food and water. An irrational part of me thought that if it survived MS too would survive, taking a leaf (pun unintended) from O. Henry's famous short story 'The Last Leaf'.

29.4.13

I marvelled at MS's resilience, for he was raring to go to his precious clinic the day after chemo, though the driver Jagdish's pay was another expense he ill tolerated. They did not get along well and I was constantly patching up their differences. MS was sore with Jagdish for banging his car twice and Jagdish was sore with MS for locking the car, pocketing the key and making him sit in the clinic lest he drive away somewhere on his own and increase the petrol bill. Though I too would have liked Jagdish to keep an eye on MS, he hated the medicinal smell.

30.4.13

My pigeon patient was improving. The wing was healing, though he walked with a limp. It was heartening to see him peck at the rice and drink water from a bowl.

Jagdish wanted to resign because MS scolded him for scratching the car against the gate when they returned at ten last night. Neighbours came out thinking that MS had caught a thief, which humiliated Jagdish even further. The days of subservient helps were gone. We had to handle them with kid gloves if we wanted their services. Going to the clinic during chemo was bad enough but going without a driver would be disastrous, so once again Amrit and I pacified Jagdish as best we could. We told MS that he would have to let go, though I knew that for him, handing over his WagonR to someone was like handing over his mistress to another. I could not touch a button or open a door of what I called his 'Mercedes' without his permission, which was ridiculous as I had been driving for eight years before he even learnt to drive. I humoured him, for he was a nervous driver and I did not want to disturb his equilibrium on the few occasions I travelled in his car.

1.5.13

A week later we arrived at the cancer hospital for the second day of the first cycle of MS's chemo. Having got the hang of it during the first time, everything went smoothly. I got him admitted in time, and as it was only one drug this time, I was hopeful the chemo would finish early. As at SSCH after his surgery, he would feign weakness and speak with me in a feeble voice from the hospital bed when he wanted something done and the next moment would talk loud and clear on the phone to his patients or compounder with the chemo drip running.

MS did have the knack of negating any sympathy I began to develop for him. He was mean enough to deny me the services of his driver, even if the driver was sitting idle. He again made me beg for the money I had to deposit for his chemo, money that he got from the joint insurance for which I too had paid in equal measure. I stood before him with a glacial stare till he peeled the notes painfully from his wallet as if he were peeling off his skin. All this took time, delaying his admission. What happened to the 'hurry' now?

In the hurry, I had forgotten my cell phone at home. As it was essential, I had to go back in his car with his driver to retrieve it. This did not go down well with him but he dared not scold me in front of his sister. An extreme lassitude engulfed me when I reached home. I lay down for a catnap, secure in the knowledge that Amrit was with him in the hospital. Barely had I closed my eyes when Bhabiji rang up to enquire about MS's health. It was a polite call that meant nothing, for when I told her that Amrit was planning to ask her and Reena to help me with MS's chemo, the response was not positive. I had learnt not to expect anything from anyone, not even our sons, and let it pass. Come to think of it, Amrit had no responsibilities towards her family (all her children were married and settled) and could very well stay on for an indefinite period, but neither did she volunteer nor did I ask her to. MS was not Bhabiji's concern; moreover, how could I take offence at her reluctance, when our own sons did not think of taking leave to be by his side. MS was my cross and I would have to bear it alone.

I returned to the hospital with tea in a thermos and snacks, which I had with Amrit. This time we were free by 2 p.m. I bought the medicines for home from a chemist outside at cheaper rates than the one in the hospital. Though MS was served lunch in daycare, despite being a diabetic, I could not eat mine due to the running around.

3.5.13

It was the eve of our wedding anniversary. Thirty-nine years ago, on this day MS had come with a baraat to my house and the marriage was solemnised the next morning. As my days as a married woman were numbered, I went with Amrit to the market to buy a lovely orange georgette gown to celebrate the day. No cancer was going to dampen my exuberance. I also baked a cake, which we cut when MS returned from his clinic. The taste of the hot, freshly baked cake was out of this world. No present, no word of appreciation awaited me.

4.5.13

I dressed up for our marriage anniversary in the flowing orange georgette sheath, put flowers in my hair and wore corals around my neck. MS didn't notice, as usual. His sister nudged him to say something nice to me but he kept mum. I was hurt by his indifference when I should have got used to it by now. Our children too did not ring us up. Perhaps they wondered what there was to celebrate in a dysfunctional marriage with the pall of a cancer hanging over it. Despite our huge differences, we were still together and that was no mean feat. For those who got along well, each day of the marriage was a celebration. The least MS could have done was to thank me for taking care of him.

5.5.13

I went with MS and Amrit to see our first movie together after his operation. Afterwards he picked up a petty quarrel with me over a small wooden cupboard that housed my precious books as he wanted to keep his medicines in it. He was nasty, mean and selfish, like his father. His mother had found a way to cope with her disastrous marriage by ignoring his father completely and finding solace in religion. Initially, I was horrified at her lack of concern for her husband's well-being but with time I learnt that he deserved to be treated with indifference. The hypochondriac had never ceased whining ever since she was married to him at the age of twelve. I could not ignore MS with his dreadful disease. His father had had a devoted elder son to look after him, while MS had only me. Keeping him alive would be keeping alive the semblance of the 'normalcy' I had known for thirty-nine years. One tends to hold on to the familiar.

Before Amrit left she tipped Sauruv handsomely to look after MS's needs. She set a timetable for MS's dietary requirements and would ring up Sauruv from Bengaluru to make sure that he was following instructions.

6.5.13

Strange how the world gets coloured by the glasses you wear. A pregnant woman will hear frightening tales of labour complications wherever she goes. As for me, I heard cancer stories. A sweet mother and son duo had come from Nepal because of the mother's gynaecological problem. I learnt that the son had early bladder cancer for which he returned every three months to our obnoxious Dr AS at SSCH. He said I was the best doctor that he had come across. Anyone would appear nice after AS but I was pleased, nevertheless. A colleague told me about a relative with advanced bladder cancer who died during chemo. Scary.

7.5.13

That MS and I were not on the best of terms was an open secret in the family. This prompted Amrit to come again and again to observe first-hand whether this lack of harmony affected my behaviour as a caregiver. How could I be anything but caring? Only an utterly vile person would plunge the dagger of revenge into the defeated, defenceless dying heart of one cursed with cancer. Satisfied by the way I was looking after her brother, she went away reassured.

Ironically, after she had been caught with an unsuitable boy in her teens, a hurried marriage had been arranged with a 'good' man with buck teeth. His prosaic nature clashed vehemently with her romantic one and she spent the rest of her life trapped in a loveless marriage. Though he showed his attachment by naming his new enterprise after her and was generous with his money, she recoiled at his touch after performing the duty of providing him with offspring. Years later when MS was long dead and gone, her husband had blood cancer and he was in and out of the ICU. They lived with their son, who took over the financial responsibility, but she had to look after the day-to-day needs of a husband she merely tolerated for appearances' sake. I would have liked to see how she was coping. Bottling up feelings never did anyone good and I suspect she succumbed to depression as she would answer in monosyllables whenever I rang up.

I returned from a night call and found Choco fast asleep on my bed. Stupidly I bent to kiss him on the forehead. Startled, he did what any animal would do – he attacked and almost bit off my nose! I screamed but MS continued to snore peacefully on his side of the bed. I was bleeding profusely and there was an ugly gash on the right side of my nose. My face throbbed and my head ached. I had to wake up MS for first aid and a tetanus shot, whether he liked it or not, and got a scolding for messing with Choco but not an iota of sympathy.

8.5.13

Amrit rang up MS twice a day to check on his progress. She was alarmed to learn that he had loose motions. It does happen at times and he was taking the requisite medicines. After putting down the phone MS told me that he did not tell her about my wounded face pulsating with pain. How would it matter to either of them? He did not care enough and she would not care as long as it did not interfere with the care of her brother, who did not care about my welfare.

Now with the changed situation, after giving so much to MS during his illness there took birth in my breast the saplings of expectations, which did me no good. If he had held me to his breast and uttered comforting words after Choco's nasty bite, it would have cost the miser nothing but would have meant the world to me. Not a single reassuring word did he utter despite the fact that he was a doctor and I a wife of thirty-nine years.

As my face was swollen and hurting, I refrained from my favourite pastime, swimming. There was an angry red scar on my face that intrigued passers-by.

9.5.13

MS had become weak. His hands trembled but he pretended that all was well lest I stop him from going to the clinic. He had even restarted the renovation that had to be stopped midway when cancer struck.

The injured pigeon I had rescued had improved vastly. Its right leg was useless and there was a tear in one wing which was healing. I brought him to the terrace so that he could make short sorties before I set him free but the feisty fellow flew to the jamun tree in front with a powerful flap of its wings. It was gratifying to see him strong and healthy, able to fend for himself. He sat his single foot on a branch grooming himself for a long while and was no longer there when I returned from work three hours later. Next day, I saw it hopping on one foot near our colony gate. A few days later I saw a dead pigeon on its back with its foot curled up. I wondered if I had done the poor fellow any good by prolonging his life by a few days.

10.5.13

The driver did not turn up. This did not deter MS, who insisted on driving to the clinic himself. Exasperated, I sent the servant along and did the cooking myself.

12.5.13

A cousin was coming from abroad and asked if I needed diapers for MS, which I did. She had a lot left over from her father-in-law, who had expired recently. Such were the presents we appreciated these days.

15.5.13

Everyone who wished me on my birthday asked, 'So how are you going to spend the day?'

'I will be sitting by my husband, while he undergoes chemo,' I replied, which left them uncomfortable, but it was true. It was the first day of the second cycle of MS's chemo. I wondered if he would give me the five thousand rupees he gave every year or plead that his chemo expenses were way too high, but he did. Not only was the cycle of chemo repeated, so was the cycle of his reluctance to part with his money.

When we met Dr Verma for the pre-admission consult, MS asked him if we could attend a wedding we were invited to later in the week. 'Yes,' he replied, 'provided, you eat only what comes out hot from the oven. No salads, cut fruits, yogurt, etc.'

'What about pizza? It comes out of a very hot oven,' I piped in, adding, 'today is my birthday.'

'Go ahead,' he said after wishing me.

'And movies?'

'Live as near a normal life as possible.'

'And whisky?' asked MS, stretching it too far, but it would be served at the wedding and there was no harm in asking. At the most it would be a no.

'A glass of wine perhaps, no more,' the doctor conceded. Life seemed good once again after the prolonged exile from normal living.

As Amrit had gone back, Ruby would be giving me company at the hospital. We had a mini feast as she had brought an almond cake and patties, which we had with coffee from the hospital canteen. She also gave me a phulkari suit and updated me on the latest regarding the criminal and civil case against her brother-in-law and the illegal occupant of their upper storey. She left with her husband at 2.30 p.m. For some reason MS seemed relieved. It was because he had wet his bed extensively and was ashamed, trying to cover the spreading patch with his blanket. His shirt and vest were totally wet at the back. The soggy diaper lay discarded on the floor. The discharge formalities over, we stepped out of the air conditioning into the merciless May heat. As we were getting into the car, I got a call from the aggressive, intimidating GM of my hospital asking me to attend a meeting. I tried telling her about my situation but she insisted. I dared not refuse the formidable lady, so I went reluctantly only to realise that the cruel can be kind too. She had learnt that it was my birthday today and had ordered a fresh fruit cake! I was deeply touched. As she handed me the knife to cut the cake, I told her to place it on the table for superstition had it that taking it directly from someone would lead to a quarrel (perhaps because it could cause injury if handed the wrong way). Well aware of her reputation, she said, '*Kaun hai jisse meri ladai nahin hue* (Who is there with whom I have not fought)!'

That night I went to Pizza Hut with MS, where we had garlic bread, sweet lime juice, fish fingers and a pizza between us. All said and done, it was not a bad birthday at all.

21.5.13
I dressed in a sequined chiffon sari for the much-anticipated wedding we were to attend. Our first fun outing after months. To my dismay I got MS's CBC report as I was readying to leave. The lab had sent it earlier but the nurse forgot to give it to me. My heart sank. TLC was just 2700 and neutrophils 34! I unwound my sari, took off my jewellery and waited with a vacant stare for MS to come home. Going to such a large gathering with such a low count was suicidal but MS was a foodie and he had looked forward to attending a lavish party after so long. He would be sorely disappointed. Hoping against hope, I tried to contact the medical oncologist in charge of MS's case three times but he would not pick up the phone. Unlike obstetricians, they are not constantly attached to their cell phones.

On his return MS began berating me for I was not dressed up in party wear. Silently I handed him the report. He began to cry, which made me cry too, at which he lashed out at me and, as usual, any desire to console him evaporated.

22.5.13
We went with the reports to ACH to meet Dr Verma. He cancelled this round of chemotherapy and asked us to buy Religrast 300 and give MS two subcutaneous injection at twenty-four-hour intervals and come again on Saturday, the 25th. It was an expensive drug and cost a thousand rupees less in the open market and though I did a lot of running around on that blistering May afternoon it was out of stock and we had to buy it from the hospital. I gave him one shot there and then so that the '24 hours later' came earlier and his WBC would increase faster.

25.5.13
The TLC had increased to 21,600 and neutrophils to 84 with Religrast. The chemo started late, at about 11.30 a.m., but as

there was only one drug therapy today after pre-medication, it was over by 3 p.m. This was the first chemotherapy session when I was alone with MS. I updated my diary and read the newspaper when I wasn't tending to him.

I don't know why I am exhausted after each chemotherapy session. Maybe, besides the physical running around, the mental and emotional stress adds up. Both of us sleep as if we have returned from a mountaineering expedition. Saturday OPD, which used to be full till now, had decreased drastically ever since the powers that be gave a parallel OPD to a new doctor they favoured and instructed the Front Office staff to direct every walk-in patient to her. I was never into corporate politics and could never understand why they put all their eggs in one basket. They promoted the highest revenue earner through aggressive marketing strategies as the face of their institution (I was perhaps the tip of its tail), though more often than not, their blue-eyed girl would walk off with the eggs, basket and all, to another more lucrative post elsewhere. Neither did I butter up the bosses nor did I indulge in networking, which formed the backbone of modern practice. Earlier, I would use the time needed for such activities following my passion for writing and now it was spent in catering to MS's cancer.

Being a good clinician, a skilled surgeon and a compassionate doctor were just not enough. Loyalty and integrity were redundant virtues in a revenue-driven enterprise and I was not all that driven. But giving my prime time and new patients that should have rightfully come to me to another was just not done. I made a last-minute bid to salvage my position.

We had been practically reduced from a double-income to a single-income family unit with doubled expenses. I met the GM and told her that I had been running Saturday OPD since the day the hospital started eleven years ago. She could give the newcomer some other evening OPD as it would make no difference to the hospital income. As MS's cancer was no secret, I also told her of my dire need for a steady income, forgetting that sympathy was not something they possessed.

'Don't try to blackmail me emotionally,' she said. 'Just because someone cries in my office it does not mean that I give in to her demands.' Though I wasn't exactly crying. Humiliated, I rushed out of her office. Never again would I beg for anything from this heartless world. If I could have I would have resigned that very instant, but there was no way I could forgo a running practice at this precarious stage of our lives.

How could I have forgotten I had a head injury in this very hospital because the light on the stairs towards their parking lot was fused. I fell down and split my head on their chipped marble step. This led to an admission, a CT scan and eight stitches on my scalp. I developed a frozen shoulder, for which I needed prolonged physiotherapy, yet it never crossed my mind to sue the hospital for compensation. A month later, they reminded me that my hospitalisation fees were pending. No colleague stood by me, but I was not going to take it lying down. Though my husband had warned me not to take on a corporate – *jal mein reh ke magarmach se vair nahin lena chahiye* (You cannot make enemies with a crocodile if you have to live in the water) – I was determined. Fuelled by outrage, I entered the director's office with my chequebook and a stinging poem I had written on the cavalier treatment meted out to me. It earned me a hefty rebate and a smiling request to write a nicer poem on their hospital the next time.

I seemed to be at odds with the entire world – MS, Rajan, my hospital, my children for leaving me alone with their ailing, insufferable father, my sister for not being the support she promised she would be. After the showdown with Rajan, I schooled myself not to depend on him for anything, even if it was long-distance emotional succour. I had learnt the hard way that expectations were the source of all unhappiness. He was based in Mumbai these days and could stay there forever for all I cared. Now that I decided to have nothing to do with him, he came to Delhi on some business and rang up asking for a glimpse of me. Glimpse, my foot! What about the umpteen glimpses he could have got when he came specially for Ruby's case, when I needed him during the most acute crisis in my life?

He said, 'Just as you cannot leave a caesarean to humour me, I could not leave them at this crucial juncture to visit you.'

Indeed! He could leave his work, spend on air tickets and fly back to Delhi interrupting his 'caesarean' whenever there was a court hearing in Ruby's case and go back without meeting me! I had had enough and told him so.

'You are strong,' he had the audacity to say. 'I know you can manage on your own. It is poor MH I am worried about.'

'Poor' MH was a 5'11" 64-year-old Sikh with a grey beard. I knew that it was Ruby he was trying to impress and not her husband. He had made me vulnerable and dependent in the earlier days and dropped me like a hot potato when I lost interest in physical intimacy due to decreasing hormones and increasing stress. If that was all that bound us, I was better off out of such a relationship.

As for MS, he was once again up to his old tricks. He had the gall to put off the AC at night again. Why didn't he understand that he was totally at my mercy and needed to humour me? I got up wretched with the heat and lack of sleep and put on the AC. Cancer or no cancer he had the energy to get up and switch it off again. When I screamed at him, he began a monologue about the electricity bill.

'That is all you think of?' I asked, enraged. 'What about the drain you have been on my pocket? What about the insurance money?' I had promised myself that I would not mention it but I had had enough of him and his electricity bill. 'I knew that you had pocketed it, but I said not a word because I felt so sorry for you, but this is the limit. How can you grudge me a few hours of restful sleep?'

27.5.13

When Amrit rang up, I snatched the phone from MS and complained about the abominable behaviour of her darling brother. I don't know what she said to him but after that day he never said a word about the AC. Perhaps the two had decided it was not wise to antagonise me when I was his sole anchor.

30.5.13

MS woke up with a 101 degree fever, frightening me no end. The doctor told me to give him a tablet of Crocin and Ciprobid. Despite this he insisted on going to his clinic. Exposing himself to infected patients was far too dangerous but nothing could dissuade him. The fever subsided in the afternoon but recurred to a lesser degree in the evening. He tried to hide the fact from his sister, but I informed her and she began to cry. She really missed their elder brother, for he would have known how to manage the stubborn younger brother.

12.6.13

While waiting for Dr Verma, I met Dr Dasgupta, a very senior gynaecologist who had earlier worked at SSCH. I told her about my husband's cancer and Dr AS's rude behaviour.

She said that she had spent a horrible ten years with him. 'Getting out of there was the best decision of my life,' she said.

The hospital was now almost a second home, the formalities routine and sitting by MS's bed, second nature. We would come early so that we could choose the best bed by a large window that overlooked a green lawn and would not be disturbed by people going up and down the aisle. MS now changed into full hospital attire, though most daycare patients preferred to remain in their home clothes. We had our reasons. His diaper overflowed rapidly due to the rapid inflow of IV fluids and the leakage would spread right up to his upper back. To avoid the embarrassment of going to the common toilet in wet garments plastered to his back, he took to changing his diaper by his bed. This led to a puddle of urine on the floor which I had to step over to gather his belongings from the bedside locker before going home.

In the entire daycare ward with twenty-five-odd beds, I heard not a cry, nor a single lament. People who came here were inured to the disease and passive acceptance prevailed. They bore their travails with stoic resignation. After the initial shock, the resilience of human nature helped in adjusting to the disease as long as it did not interfere seriously with day-to-day living. The dying process had not actively begun yet and it was simpler to live in the present. We all went through the motions of admission, watching the drip, calling the nurse to change the bottle or when the drops stopped falling to flush out the clots from the cannula and also to begin the discharge formalities with the ease of routine. Perhaps that is why the plaintive cry, '*bawli tera bhai mar reha hai*', by a patient on the adjoining bed to his sister, struck a discordant note. This reminded me of a lady doctor with ovarian cancer who would sob hysterically and exclaim that she did not want to die. MS never said a word.

As I busied myself looking after MS, adjusting his pillows, raising the head end of his bed when lunch came, adjusting the napkin around his neck, he gave me a look of pure unadulterated love, the first in thirty-nine years of marriage! It warmed me to my depths. I was sick myself with gastroenteritis (I even had a copious vomit here) but was not allowed to lie down on the vacant bed by his side as the afternoon shift of chemo patients would be arriving soon.

These days I was reading the *Tibetan Book of Living and Dying*. It gave me much solace. It prepared me for death, his or mine, whichever came first, and taught me how to help the dying make their exit peacefully. Though I did not become enlightened enough to practise Tolgen – giving and receiving, with infinite compassion; taking in the suffering of all others and giving them *my* positive emotions – I learnt to overlook MS's faults and treat him like a temperamental child entirely at my mercy. Perhaps I am in my element wherever I feel needed; perhaps that was why I became a doctor in the first place.

16.6.13
Mona's parents were coming over to see MS. He went to Big Bazaar to get paneer for them though I told him not to exert himself unnecessarily just to save a few rupees (we could have got it from the neighbourhood shop). As he was going by metro, I asked him to renew my metro card at the station counter; he refused. At this my voice and my blood pressure shot up. He left with a smug smile having once again managed to destroy my equilibrium. What did he stand to gain from such meanness? If it was subtle revenge he was extracting for being unfaithful to him those long years ago, what made me nurse one who had cheated me of my last penny much before that? Guilt, repentance? Why didn't I desert him when he deserved to be left? His sons and sister could bloody well look after him.

18.6.13

Why is it that a husband and wife of nearly forty years cannot speak a civil word to each other despite the fact that our lives are intertwined as vines that can only break but never unwind. One would have thought that with such an affliction looming we would have been more understanding of each other but that was not to be. MS's meanness had magnified manifold and I showed my resentment by hitting back. He could exert and expose himself to infection to save a few rupees but would plead his 'condition' whenever I asked him to do something for me. In fact, that was the only time he mentioned his 'condition'.

He was too sick to accompany me to the police station to lodge an FIR when I lost my purse with my money, debit card and driving licence in it (I was wary of going there alone), but he could go all the way to Lajpat Nagar to pay the house tax for the property of his deceased brother and refuse to do it for the flat I had recently bought in my name. How dare he blackmail me with his 'condition' to avoid doing something for me! How could he take all from me as his due and give nothing in return?

I knew that he needed nutritious food but not a piece of liver, not a drop of chicken soup, not a slice of boiled egg or exotic fruit would he share with me. Did he not understand that keeping his caregiver healthy was as important if he wanted to be well looked after?

19.6.13

As the driver was ill, I drove MS to the hospital. My morning swim had delayed me a bit and MS was in a boil, which made my blood boil, and a mighty quarrel ensued. What a pair we made! It was difficult to understand how if he earned such a substantial amount from his clinic a delay of a few minutes would impact his income. Where was all the money going? Why was he always cribbing about money?

His blood report showed haemoglobin 8.7 g/dL and the doctor advised us to arrange for a transfusion to counteract the anaemia before his next chemo session. A distant relative donated blood though Ruby had said that her son and daughter-in-law would donate if we needed it again. Thankfully, the doctor had written the admission and blood transfusion instructions before he left for the rounds, which saved us an hour. Chemo was over by 2.30 p.m. and so was our lunch but not the blood transfusion. Though I should have got used to it by now, I continued to be hurt by our kids' indifference. They seemed not to care to learn whether MS had tolerated the transfusion or the chemo well. Neither of them rang up to find out.

23.6.13

MS's illness did not prevent him from going to the wholesale market in Mongolpuri to buy tiles for his clinic. He lost a bundle of fifty- and hundred-rupee notes while paying for them and took out his anger on me. When I tried to express my concern, he shouted, '*Do mint chup nahin reha janda hai tere kol* (Can't you keep quiet for two minutes)?'

I couldn't help saying, 'When do we ever talk with each other?'

'I want to go over events and concentrate on thinking where I could have lost my money.'

Indeed! His money lost was to be treated with the gravity of a funeral while my lost purse with ten thousand rupees, debit cards and driving licence did not warrant a single sympathetic word. Heaven and hell are on earth and one gets a taste of one's own medicine sooner or later, in this very lifetime.

In the BC (before cancer) days we usually walked through Shakurpur market on the way to Samrat cinema because the movie tickets and the vegetables we bought on our way back were cheap. I'd pause every now and then to take pictures of this vibrant marketplace, much to MS's annoyance.

The place was like a tightly packed miniature city pulsating with life; people amiably shared space with ambling cattle, darting goats, dogs and cats and scurrying rats. I loved watching fresh vegetables and fruit piled on the ground or on pushcarts, multihued spices, haldi, mirchi, garam masala heaped like the colours of Holi. There were cheap trinkets, readymade clothes, belts and bags for the lower class. There were colourful glass bangles, which I was not averse to buying. There were gol guppas, chat papdi, kachori and tikki stalls. Hot, juicy jalebis and spicy samosas emerged from large woks filled with reused oil of dubious origin, as did fried fish and chicken tikka at another stall. There was even a man with a large cauldron into which he delved to scoop large scoopfuls of chicken pulao for the crowd that gathered around his cart. The only thing I ever ate from this surging market was corn cobs freshly roasted on live coals during the monsoons.

I always averted my eyes when we reached the far end of the market. Here sat butchers with live chicken in coops that they slaughtered as and when required. There were fish vendors with live fish in tubs that were taken out to die for us. Though I ate non-vegetarian food with relish, I could not bear to see them being killed – a paradox difficult to explain.

We had resumed our routine of going to the movies on Sundays. I had assumed we would go to a cleaner, expensive theatre in a mall as it would reduce chances of infection, which was of paramount importance during chemo, but the only concession MS made to his disease was to wear a mask. Also, for the first few times we sat segregated from the crowd in the box of the old-fashioned single-screen cinema hall. We were later barred from going there as it was reserved for family members of the theatre owner and open to public only when the house was full. Today it was just the two of us. It felt like a home theatre, so much so that when I received a phone call from the hospital during the show, I asked MS to turn the volume down just as I did at home!

Samrat played an important part in our lives. Having lived with a miser all my life, I got accustomed to a frugal lifestyle and even began to emulate him in certain matters. The popcorn tasted as good if not better and was cheaper too. Ever since they had stopped serving coffee, we shared a bottle of Pepsi between us with a separate straw for the caffeine kick. I did not mind as both of us were diabetics. So to Samrat we went every Sunday evening through the filth and squalor of the Shakurpur Sunday market. I began taking my car with the windows shut tight to prevent infection. As I manoeuvred my vehicle on these precarious roads, narrowed by encroachments, clogged with people and pushcarts, dogs and donkeys, cattle and cats, honking my way through, MS's compulsive back seat driving drove me mad. A massive quarrel ensued and neither of us spoke a word to each other in the theatre.

My heart was heavy with unshed sorrow, for added to personal woes was the sad ending of the movie *Ranjhana*. When cheerful, the threshold for laughter decreases as it does for tears when sad, which is why, quite unreasonably, the sight of a flowering frangipani in a cracked pot near the car park made me want to cry. The fresh white flowers, framed by dark green leaves, bloomed courageously, belying their impending doom.

3.7.13

Jessy turned six months old today and while they celebrated in Bengaluru, the mood in this household was sombre, for, as usual, every important day in our family calendar was spent in the hospital. We had managed to get the same bed by the large glass window. MS has settled on it for day one of the fourth cycle of chemo. I sit on the same chair by his side watching the lethal drops drip into his vein. Chemo drugs kill all fast-growing cells, be they cancerous or normal, which results in severe side effects and an increased susceptibility to infection due to immuno-suppression. I have to remain vigilant and call the nurse before the fluid in the bottle finishes to prevent air embolism and death. Hence, I dare not grab my forty winks while my poor cancer-ridden husband snores peacefully. It reminds me of the song in the movie *Milan – 'main jaagu, tu so jaye'*.

7.7.13
MS has a 101 degree fever. His skin is cold and clammy, he bathes with hot water in this hot and humid weather, feels weak and yet, against medical advice, he has been overexerting himself by going to the school again, an hour before his clinic. He had been doing a preventive health check-up of schoolchildren for years and had joined back after recovering from prostate surgery. This was followed by a full OPD and the renovation of his clinic and he drove the car reaching home by 2.30 p.m. Such long hours in such humid weather would deplete any normal person but his will was stronger than his flesh. Perhaps he wanted to wear himself out to death before cancer dragged him down by the collar. But this means that much more work for me. I am fed up with this morbid cycle but see no way out. I rang up Amrit and informed her of his foolish obstinacy. She scolded him for overdoing things, at which he scolded me for carrying tales.

In dire need of entertainment, we saw a movie, *Lootera*, which was much too serious for his liking. I was alarmed to see him shiver with just the fan on. It was to a sorry, sombre household we returned. We slept on our double bed just a few feet apart, facing away from each other. No two lonelier souls lived under one roof.

Neither of my brothers in the US and UK rang up to ask after MS's health, his chemo and how I was coping alone. Though one of them had flown with his wife from the US to look up his ailing 87-year-old father-in-law in Nagpur (MS was only 67), he did not come to visit us in Delhi. Karan never rang up on chemotherapy days, neither did he seem overly bothered when I told him that his father had fever. Except for Amrit, no one cared whether we lived or died.

I catered to MS's idiosyncrasies, lay next to him in a urine-soaked bed and woke up night after night to clean it. It never occurred to me to shift to another room but, after all these relentless months, descending the lows with MS and no sympathy or help from any quarter, a meltdown was inevitable. I had begun to suffer from caregiver's burnout, but I forced myself to come up for air. I could not afford the luxury of giving in to despair when MS's very life depended upon my ministrations.

8.7.13

MS seemed to be going his brother's way. Both his father and elder brother had COPD, chronic obstructive airways disease. While his father barely moved, thereby exerting his compromised lungs minimally, he lived the life of a semi-invalid till the ripe old age of ninety-four. The brother, on the other hand, overworked his incapacitated lungs, getting breathless every so often, till they gave up on him at the age of sixty-nine. Perhaps MS had a subconscious death wish, but Amrit and I would not let go that easily. She wanted Simar to confront his father and drive some sense into him, which I thought was unnecessary, for Simar had just been transferred to Mumbai and it was not feasible to take leave so soon. In desperation, I rang up the doctor and told him that MS insisted on going to the clinic despite his fever. He scolded MS roundly, ordered him to stay at home and get a CBC done for his counts may have decreased.

17.7.13

Today, I got a scary preview of the future. As I was getting off the lift after my evening OPD at the hospital, an emaciated black-bearded Sikh entered the lift in a wheelchair. Uncannily he began calling out, 'Rosy, Rosy,' which was my pet name too, and a woman ran to join him before the lift doors closed and he was pacified.

24.7.13

Though MS was on a diet of iron-rich foods, he could not tolerate iron tablets and his haemoglobin dropped to 8.8 g/dL. As he was due for chemo, his doctor suggested a blood transfusion first. After admission, I covered him with a white sheet till his chest as usual so that he could undergo chemo without the embarrassment of a visible urinary leak.

Today the daycare chemo ward looked like the cancer ward I had always imagined; instead of the peace and quiet that prevailed during our previous visits there were sounds of wails and cries all around. A thick needle had pierced the abdominal wall of a patient with a swollen belly for an ascitic tap. It was full of ascitic fluid that pressed against his diaphragm, leading to breathlessness. Though drainage of litres of the straw-coloured liquid would lead to protein depletion, it could be replaced. This was mere palliation to make breathing easy for the terminally ill as the abdomen would fill up again soon enough. A bone marrow biopsy was being performed on a child and his screams pierced my heart. I prayed for all these stricken patients in general and for my husband in particular and hoped he would not have to suffer so.

'God please look after him,' I beseeched. The cancer had bonded us in a way that no other bond could. Even as these bittersweet thoughts were coursing through my mind, lunch arrived. After raising the head end of his bed, spreading the napkin, filling a glass of water and settling him in a comfortable position to eat, I opened my lunch box to eat along with him. As the food from home was too dry to swallow, I asked MS for a bit of gravy from his hospital lunch. He looked at me as if I was snatching milk from a child's mouth and refused outright.

'I will need the rajma to eat with rice after eating chapattis and vegetables,' he said self-righteously. Seeing the look on my face, he tried to crack a joke but I was not amused. There was a lump in my throat. Unable to control my tears, I went to the veranda, rested my head on the railing and wept bitterly. Passers-by thought I was crying for my cancer-stricken relative when I was crying because of him.

Purged of hurt and hatred, at least for the moment, I returned once again to sit by his bed. Raising his bed or lowering it as demanded, giving him water, covering him, pulling out his slippers from under the bed when he wanted to use the toilet and watching over the infusion bottles like a hawk to prevent air embolism. As the stay today was longer than usual, due to blood transfusion, he was sedated. The urine patch on his bed had spread to reach his torso. Tea came in the evening with two Marie biscuits. Perhaps he felt ashamed of his behaviour in the afternoon for he offered me one biscuit. After this, I wiped his back with a wet towel, helped him change into his street clothes, removed his patka, helped him put on his turban, packed his belongings, swallowed my pride and begged for money, to complete the discharge formalities. Then I drove home and tucked him into bed.

MS's apparent lack of concern about his disease never ceases to amaze. Like a clockwork toy, he goes to his clinic and back as if that was the sole purpose of his existence. At other times, I admire his spirit and am glad that he does not indulge in introspection or self-pity. During the day he appears normal (the full-sleeved shirt and pants cover his wasted limbs), it is easy to delude myself that all is well and embark upon our chronic quarrels to give our marriage a semblance of the 'old normal'.

The disease had begun to affect us mentally, and mutual irritability had increased exponentially. Now that chemo cycles were almost over and he would soon be free of his dependence on me, he was back to his old obnoxious ways with a vengeance. He woke me up during my catnap in the afternoon. When I reprimanded him, he said, '*Shor na macha,*' as if I was an uncouth villager who knew no better than to talk back to her lord and master. He had used this phrase during his BC days when I asked him a question as he was ineffectively trying to manoeuvre his car during rush hour. I let it pass then, for I knew he was just taking out the stress of his inefficient driving on that occasion.

'You say this once again and then you see,' I threatened. I did not know what I would make him see, but it worked. Finally, I learnt the meaning of the adage *Be careful what you tolerate. You are teaching people how to treat you.*

21.8.13

Uncannily MS's chemo fell on festival dates, birthdays, anniversaries. This time it was on Rakhi. Sentimentally, Amrit came all the way from Bengaluru to tie the sacred thread around her brother's wrist. God knows how many more brother–sister festivals they would get to share; this was the first after the diagnosis. So we went through the entire works – ardaas, photos, tying of rakhi and mithai. MS gave her eleven hundred rupees, which was way less than what she had spent on the airfare to be with him. She had also got two T-shirts for him. As she complained about his stinginess, it was on the tip of my tongue to tell her that I had been subjected to such behaviour all my married life, but that would put her on the defensive. What she wanted was consolation, so I commiserated with her and made MS give another thousand.

Whenever I complained of MS's stinginess to anyone in the family, they would tell me, 'It is your personal matter, sort it out yourself.' But when I took solace where I could find it – in another man's arms – they came forward in droves to condemn me. Why wasn't I allowed to sort *this* personal matter myself?

When MS's miserliness extended to others, like Amrit today, paradoxically, they appealed to me for help. Years ago, MS had offered to buy air tickets for my father at a cheaper rate and assured them that the agent would meet them with the tickets at the airport. My elderly parents waited in vain that cold winter night, with their twin grandchildren, for the agent and my father had to finally buy new tickets. I was horrified to hear about this from my father of course, but a nasty part of me wanted to say, 'It's between you and him, don't involve me.'

Years later, with MS long dead and gone, history repeated itself. We were stranded with his (our) grandchildren at Jim Corbett because a patient in a high post in the railway ministry had promised me return rail tickets and ditched us at the last moment. We ended up hiring a Tempo Traveller at exorbitant rates and suffered an uncomfortable fifteen-hour road journey, suffocated by pollution and traffic jams. The Shatabdi would have taken a mere six hours with food and drinks thrown in. MS's family had to suffer for his sins even after his death.

My brother came from the US to deliver a prestigious talk and put up at Ruby's place. Though I went there for Rakhi, he would only get to meet MS at a family get-together at a restaurant that evening. He was shocked at the change in MS's appearance. Scrutinising him through my brother's eyes, I was saddened to see his white beard and wasted body, with a head and turban too big for his frail neck to carry. 'He looks like Manmohan Singh,' whispered my brother in my ear, which brought a smile to our faces.

23.8.13

Usually, when Amrit came for a holiday, she would go to meet Bhabiji in Nainital and her sister's daughter Reena in Chandigarh. This time, wanting to be near her brother for as long as possible, she called them to Delhi. Though I liked their company and would have been happy to receive them at any other time, I had too much on my hands now. Playing hostess would be an additional burden. As if this was not enough, she called over her Delhi cousins too, whom I had kept at bay till now. It was just like the time when her parents were alive and the entire clan would descend from the hills to escape the harsh winter there. They would live with us for months right in the thick of my children's exams. To cap it their Delhi relatives would come to visit them and mayhem would prevail.

Paradoxically, though MS's disease stressed me, thoughts of a future without him stressed me more and these two-pronged worries were driving me mad. Senior citizens living alone, more so a single woman, were soft targets, chiefly for predatory servants turned potential murderers overnight. I had shared a major part of my life with MS, though the sharing was now reduced to sleeping with our back towards each other on two sides of a double bed – he on a mackintosh and me on a bed of thorns, separated by an ocean of silence. Yet the mere presence of a man in the household, however debilitated, was enough to ward off predators. I remembered the story of a man with partial paralysis who worked in a bank. His wife and three lovely daughters looked after him with genuine concern. One day when a glass of milk fell from his wasted hand, he told his wife, 'I will be serving your purpose better dead than alive.' She would get his pension and a job at the bank. To which she had replied, 'Even a man's shoes outside the threshold means security for a family of women. We are protected from the eyes of predatory men as long as you are alive, and that is all that matters.'

27.8.13
MS came home early as he had a backache. This was alarming, for nothing would make him miss his clinic. I worried about bone metastasis but did not voice my concern. As MS's blood reports were normal, we would be going for his last chemo tomorrow. This time the date fell on Janmashtami. MS hoped that there would be no swimming on this account but I had to disappoint him. I do not know what he had against my swimming when, by keeping myself fit, I was serving his purpose too.

28.8.13
MS woke me up earlier than usual to ask if I would go for a swim, when it had been confirmed yesterday that the pool would be open. Needling people was a sport he inherited from his father. Both got a perverse pleasure from it. Not having slept enough, I entered the pool with a pounding head. I managed to return in time for his chemo session, but as luck would have it, a long Janmashtami procession passed by our house. Though we had the good fortune to see the idols of Radha Krishna on a chariot and were blessed

to receive the prasad, MS looked upon the procession as an obstacle for we could not take the car out.

Despite MS's whining we reached earlier than most patients and got our favourite bed by the large glass window overlooking the well-tended garden. The doctor asked us to take a date for a PET scan, get MS's liver and kidney function tests done and a new test for detecting cancer cells in his urine. I was afraid, very afraid. I prayed that the tests be normal and MS was declared cancer-free so that we could live a normal existence.

Amrit and I went to the basement to get a date for the PET scan. I had stopped asking MS how much money he carried. Earlier I would tell him to carry some extra amount, but he never listened, perhaps fearing that I'd pocket it. No transaction in the hospital was complete without a receipt but it was humiliating to account for every rupee spent. Today, that extra amount was needed as an advance deposit for a PET scan, which I paid. Amrit was surprised at my breathlessness on climbing a single flight of stairs from the basement to the ward. I warned her, 'At the rate your brother tortures me, I am more likely to die of high blood pressure and a heart attack before his cancer takes its toll.' She was genuinely worried for me, though more for the sake of her brother than anything else, I think. As we sat by MS during his last chemo, I poured out my heart to Amrit.

'How do you expect me to sympathise with him when he does not care for me? Did you not notice that yesterday he bought medicines for your headache but not for my diarrhoea?'

Amrit ruefully compared him to her father, who had made life hell for her mother. She tried telling him to be nice to me, at which he put on his 'poor thing' look.

Thankfully, the last chemo was done, though it was not the end. There would be follow-ups and tests that would keep us on tenterhooks. We had won but a small battle; the moot point was for how long the war would rage before we gave up, for defeat was a given.

8.9.13

Our neighbour's son got married and the reception was being held at a five-star hotel in Connaught Place. As it was a Sunday, the shops were closed, but before we went to the hotel I wanted to stroll around the upmarket place for a bit of window shopping and pick up trinkets from the patri bazaar. MS agreed after I insisted. He bickered, his face a picture of torture as I bargained for books and pretty artificial jewellery with the pavement vendors, which was a part of the enjoyment. Within twenty minutes he herded me back into the car and we reached the venue even before the groom's and bride's relatives. Had it been a working day we would have reached by 10.30 p.m., after his clinic. He was disappointed with the vegetarian fare, no matter how rich and expensive. The least this damp squib of a party owed him was a drink. He was allowed only wine, but as it was not yet chilled, he came back from the bar triumphantly holding aloft a glass of whisky. I did not have the heart to scold him, for not a sip had passed his lips since the beginning of his chemo. I clucked over him like a mother hen as his defiance was not restricted only to the whisky. He was relishing gol guppas and chat papdi with dollops of chutney barely three weeks after his last chemo and his defences still down.

11.9.13

MS had tea and biscuits at 5.30 a.m. and slept off. I stayed awake most of the night with a fussy patient who had a seventeen-week-old malformed foetus that thankfully aborted at 5.50 a.m. However, I had to remove the retained placenta surgically. Groggy with lack of sleep, I bathed and dressed quickly as we had to reach the hospital by 8.45 a.m. for the PET scan.

As MS was in a perpetual state of hurry, we reached before the hospital staff. While waiting for them to arrive, we watched TV, skimmed through the newspapers strewn on a table in the waiting room, used the washroom, in short did everything else but communicate. I went upstairs to deposit the remaining ten thousand rupees (we had paid eight thousand in advance). By the time I returned MS was inside. I was handed his steel kara and watch by the receptionist and was called inside to take his pants and phone but to our amazement he would not part with the latter. He wanted to call his compounder to tell him that he was unable to attend the morning clinic so that patients were not kept waiting for him but the compounder would not answer. Commendable indeed, this sense of responsibility, but despite being asked twice on the speaker by the technician behind the protective screen to stop using the phone, he clung to it. I could have easily done this little chore for him. Finally, the technician came in person to snatch it from his hand and gave it to me, telling me to hurry out of this high radiation area.

12.9.13

The day passed normally enough. I was free by 9 p.m. As there was still time for dinner with the lord and master, who came late, I asked Sauruv to cut some fruit, though I knew that the apples tasted like potatoes and the guavas were cricket-ball hard as MS usually bought the cheapest. As Sauruv told me there was no fruit in the outside fridge, I rummaged through the one in the bedroom, where we kept dry fruit under lock and key lest the help filch them. Hidden in its depths I espied a large packet of juicy red apples that MS must have been helping himself to every morning before I woke up. I had learnt to compromise with the fact that he ate the liver, pomegranate, etc., for his anaemia without offering me a bite, but couldn't we have had this common fruit together?

What's in an apple, one would ask. Why was I so worked up? Couldn't I buy as many as I wanted? Why did it hurt more than the larger atrocities he inflicted upon me? It symbolised his attitude towards me – his wife, the mother of his children, his companion, his caretaker, his doctor. I wouldn't even treat domestic help in this manner.

13.9.13

I rang up Amrit to tell her that I had had enough of her beloved brother, who grudges me a measly apple!

'You know there is no love lost between us, but as a doctor and a caring human, I did not forsake him. That he cares so little for my welfare hurts. You know dieticians advice special diets for the caretakers of the chronically ill? For selfish reasons, we even humour the help. I have seen you load Sauruv with gifts in cash and kind so that he looks after your brother.'

As she was digesting this bit of information I continued, 'How can he be so short-sighted? Does he think he will not need my services now that his chemo is over and the PET scan is normal? It's just two weeks after chemo and he is stage IV. You know, Amrit, I can handle big problems, but little things like this break my heart.'

She said, 'Let bygones be bygones.'

'How could I have lived with him if I had not let bygones be bygones. As for the apples, I discovered them today!'

'*Kahan le jayega paise? Kiske liye chod ke jaane hain? Bacche dono settled hain, phir aapas me kyun nahin prem pyar se reh sakte* (Where will he take all his money, for whom will he leave it? Both children are settled and yet we cannot live amicably with each other).'

Pressing my point I added, 'Can you believe there are no onions in our salad after you left? No one would believe it that I live a life of deprivation in this house. Even Sauruv treats his wife better.'

Amrit listened quietly as I emptied the bile accumulated against MS in her ears. I do not know why I told all this to his sister (not that my sister was interested), for her sympathies lay with him. Perhaps I wanted to keep her abreast of the goings-on in my household so that she understood why I behaved so badly with her sick brother at times. I was the honest, open fighter, while he operated on the sly. I ended my tirade with 'No need to tell him about my outburst. It will serve no useful purpose.'

'OK. Let's talk of something else.'

'I forgot to tell you that he was thinking of letting go of the driver, which I think is a foolish thing to do.'

This, as expected, worried her more than my list of grievances. 'He should not. I will discuss it with him in the evening.'

When MS came home at night, he accused me of carrying tales. This meant that Amrit had not kept her word. As for the fruit, Amrit had bought it for him before she left! This meant that sister and brother were hand in glove and she had bought them solely for his consumption! What a fool I was!

That night I lay in bed, a quivering mass of misery, trying hard to call sleep to my tear-laden eyes. MS touched my shoulder and said, 'Sorry.' This hurt me more than his trying to deny his meanness, for it meant that it was not an act of omission but commission!

I had never felt so alone in my entire life. The children had left, my husband did not care whether I lived or died, while my own family had forgotten me and my troubles. I tried to cheer myself up with the thought that if no one looked after me when I fell ill, I would die sooner and wouldn't have to suffer indefinitely.

Karan came from the US for his father's sixty-seventh birthday on 25th September. I gifted MS two pairs of good quality leather shoes and decided to pay the restaurant bill for dinner at Barbeque Nation, where we would celebrate with my sister and her family, but the waiter put the bill in Karan's hand, which meant he had to pay.

With Simar away, I took Karan around during his 'holiday'. We saw the movie *Lunch Box*, went to a photo exhibition at the India Habitat Centre and visited Dilli Haat. I was thoroughly exhausted by the third day, for added to the hectic schedule was fatigue, anaemia and IBS (the episodes had become frequent and did not disappear as quickly as before). I had had it twice in recent times, each episode lasting for almost a month. The vomiting and diarrhoea could be the cause of anaemia and nutritional deficiency that left me feeling weak and tired all the time. Today I was truly alarmed to see coffee-coloured particles in the vomit, which I suspected could be altered blood. I asked Karan, a renowned GI, to look at it before I pulled the flush. He was disgusted at being called upon to view such an exhibit, though he advised me to get my stools tested for occult blood and get an endoscopy. My last experience of gastroscopy years ago was under an oily local anaesthetic that I had to swallow and then swallow a snake like scope; it was horrible but there was no point in delaying investigations, as MS had done. He was the first cancer patient in our family. Lest I become the second, I visited a GI specialist in my hospital and got a date for gastroscopy and colonoscopy, which thankfully he would do under GA.

Meanwhile, the anaemia had to be corrected. Though MS could not tolerate the slow-release iron tablets I had got for him from a medical representative, he refused to give them to me. Instead of stressing myself over such a minor issue as I would have done earlier (his nature could not change), I bought the medicines myself. Of the iron-rich fruits and goat liver, MS always took the larger share. How come his anaemia was anaemia and mine was not! As for the help who took all the samples of iron tablets I got, for kamzori (weakness), I got his haemoglobin tested too. It was 15 g/dL while mine was 9 g/dL.

8.10.13

I had an extremely hectic day at the hospital. Besides delivering women in the daytime, I had to go to the hospital again at night to operate upon a ruptured ectopic pregnancy. I had taken Exelyte to prepare my bowels for my endoscopy schedule for the next morning and was completely drained by the spurts of watery stools that I passed even in the OT before and after the surgery. Thankfully, I could control it during the procedure, though as a precaution I had put a thick wad of toilet paper in the cleft of my buttocks to prevent an embarrassing leakage. I was totally dehydrated by the time I finished the surgery. As doctors, we prescribe purgatives to patients as a routine, but today I understood their plight; however, they did not have to perform a surgery after taking it. I took a cleansing bath after I returned as I felt dirty and sticky but avoided the Alprax tablet prescribed, fearing that I might pass watery stools in bed if I passed out.

9.10.13

Got up at the unearthly hour of 5 a.m. and reached the hospital with MS at 6 a.m. I had forgotten my cell phone and we had to return to retrieve it; MS had the good sense not to scold me. When driving back home, I saw a mynah (one for sorrow), and the help had shattered a cup. These were seemingly 'bad omens' to the irrational part of my mind, which overrides the rational one in such a tense situation. I tried to overlook them but couldn't help rejoicing when, on our way back, the single mynah was joined by its partner (two for joy) and a huge red ball of sun rose over the loop flyover – a wonderful sight and the best omen ever.

It felt surreal to change into a patient's clothes and lie in the very room I entered every day as a doctor. MS waited in the doctor's lounge. Through an IV line I was given a sedative that made me pass out. I do not know when I was transferred to the trolley and wheeled into the OT. I had planned to shoo away male OT assistants during the procedure as it would be embarrassing to work with them after they had seen me naked, but the only thing I remembered was trying to pull out the gastroscope and hear someone say, 'Give her some Propofol.' I dimly recall sliding back on the bed with the help of a patient slide.

The colonoscopy was normal but the gastroscopy revealed three benign-looking polyps from which the gastroenterologist took a biopsy. I was charged for just one procedure and discharged by 12.30 p.m., slept till 3 p.m., and by evening I felt fit enough to attend my evening OPD. For once MS lent me his driver. I think I was as driven as MS as far as my work was concerned, for no amount of purgatives or anaesthetic agents could keep me away. Writing and operating were the two passions of my life.

11.10.13

Histopathology of the polyp revealed that they were due to inflammation; thankfully, no H. pylori, no neoplasia. I was vastly relieved, for the scare of cancer had kept me on tenterhooks. For that brief time, I got a taste of what MS must be going through.

20.10.13

My sister came to visit me after my 'surgery' and got about two kilos of pomegranates with ruby-red hearts. These, I told MS, were for me alone, so that he learnt how it feels when one's partner is so mean about food. Of course the help would pop some in his mouth on the sly while peeling it but that could not be helped. Sauruv had the manipulative brains of a devious genius and took full advantage of our dependence on him. When I began scolding him for something, he would divert my attention towards MS saying things like 'the lady's finger I am cutting is full of worms' and I'd end up fighting with MS for buying rotten vegetables just because they were cheap and forget about Sauruv, who would be laughing to himself in the kitchen. I caught on to his game soon enough and stopped bickering with MS at his instigation.

22.10.13
Today was Karva Chauth. Couples become all lovey-dovey, for the wife, decked in bridal glory, abstains from food and water, for the long life of her husband, and he buys her expensive gifts. MS had gone to Karol Bagh to buy his diapers and said that the chhole bhature wala 'called' him, so he had to have a plate. Similarly, the dahi bhalle wala, the fish fry wala or the chicken pulao wala would 'call' him whenever he went to the market alone, but he never got anything packed for me. I had stopped minding, for though I could not resist the spicy street food, it upset my delicate stomach. This was one of his negative traits I was grateful for, but a gift for Karva Chauth was definitely in order, as an expression of gratitude, if nothing else. When I asked if the sari shop wala or the jeweller did not lure him with Karva Chauth offers, he answered with a curt no.

The exploitation we suffered at the hands of our employees was beyond compare. As a doctor, time and again I had been kind to poor people and charged way less for services, but whenever I needed their help, they demanded atrocious amounts of money, worked shoddily and stole whatever they could without hesitation. I would turn a blind eye to petty thefts, writing them off as occupational hazards, but that was then. Now the situation had worsened. The more we needed them, the less time we had to supervise them and the more daring they became.

The latest to join the bandwagon was our nice nurse Sunita and Jagdish the driver. Jagdish was handsome in a delicate and pale sort of way with an aquiline nose and a long, narrow face. He was the only son of a woman who ironed clothes to make a living; her husband had run away with another woman when Jagdish was a year old. They lived in a rented room in a nearby village.

Though Amrit and I would take his side when MS scolded him as we wanted him to stay, MS's annoyance was justified at times. Jagdish would invariably be late for work. A couple of months into the job, much to our surprise, he began turning up before time. Sunita, the nurse on afternoon duty, was the reason. This weak character, drawn to strong women like his mother, fell head over heels in love with Sunita, with her no-nonsense air and calm efficiency. That she was five years older than him, thin and dark made no difference to him. That she would have none of him added fuel to his desire. Though she was not averse to gossiping with him, she would not marry him, for she had had a borderline malignant brain tumour in early adulthood and she had been through a brain surgery and chemotherapy. Though ten years had passed, she worried that it might recur and did not want to spoil his life, but Jagdish refused to take no for an answer. Like the spoilt child he was, he craved for what was beyond reach. That she was an educated woman, daughter of a modestly well-off agricultural landowner with a house of their own, and he was a 10th pass north Indian who lived in a rented one-room quarter did not deter him. As he was younger, fairer and better-looking than her and besotted by her, Sunita began to soften towards him. The holding of hands, the prolonged emotional conversations did not go unnoticed and soon reached my ears, chiefly through Sauruv's wife, Kamla, whose favourite pastime was playing one against the other. She had a bone to pick with Sunita for refusing to babysit her children so that she could work outside. Indeed! Sunita enjoyed playing with Kamla's kids and even got them sweets, dresses and toys, but this was asking too much. This created a rift between them and Kamla the gauche villager who had by now metamorphosed into a sly city girl thought that I would fire them. Why should I? They were unencumbered, consenting adults and could do as they wished. I chose not to confront them, which frustrated Kamla.

On the other hand, knowing that our need for him was dire, Sauruv's petty pilfering increased exponentially. Otherwise too, he ate more than the two of us and our dog put together. Now, his entire family began fattening up at our expense. Sauruv developed a paunch and Kamla's breasts began to pop out of her clothes, their skinny daughter, whom I called chippkali (being as thin and clingy as a gecko), put on flesh and their little son became positively chubby in a matter of months on my rations. I turned a blind eye to the goings-on in the larger interest of my family. I even got their daughter admitted in a government school. I also had an ulterior motive, for now Sauruv, who was quick to take offence, would not threaten to leave at the slightest pretext, as his daughter's education was at stake.

Sunita was enraged by Kamla's backbiting but when she saw that I was not annoyed by her dalliance with Jagdish, she was relieved. It wasn't as if she wanted to marry him. In fact, she was helping his mother choose a bride for him, but now that Kamla had squealed on her, Sunita began telling me what they did behind my back. When Kamla would bad-mouth us, Sunita would advise her not to speak ill of someone who had given them a roof over their heads and their daily bread.

'They earn through honest labour and give it to us with a good heart, so learn to be content. *Aisi kamai mein barkat hoti hai,*' said Sunita.

'You are a fine one to say,' replied Kamla. 'You earn more than us and have no encumbrances.'

Did she not realise that Sunita had to study hard to become a nurse, that Sunita had skills that Kamla could never even hope to aspire to, which was why she earned more.

Earlier Sauruv would rush down to deposit MS's emergency bag and water bottle in the car so that he got a few minutes to gossip with Jagdish. However, for the last couple of months Sauruv had begun saying things like, 'This is a driver's job, not mine. He should also clean the car instead of drinking tea that the nurse makes for him.'

I learnt the reason for his sudden hostility towards Jagdish from Sunita. On the days Jagdish drove us to the hospital for chemotherapy, Sauruv would quietly flick the backroom key from the peg in our room, and the moment we left, his family would settle on the double bed in the guest room, switch on the AC and the TV and have parathas with butter and curd. They would then raid the fridge I kept locked in that room and help themselves to juices and handfuls of dry fruit. I recalled then an incident that had happened a few weeks ago. Kamla's four-year-old daughter was standing in the dark by the gate with something in her mouth that she could not bite into.

'What are you eating?' I had asked.

'Moongphali.'

'Haven't you shelled the peanut? Show me,' I said, as a peanut shell wasn't that hard to crack. Out came an unshelled pistachio! Kamla hastened to exclaim, 'My brother-in-law brought them.' This was highly unlikely, but I let it pass. Now I put two and two together.

'But what was Jagdish's role in all this?' I asked, puzzled. Sunita said Jagdish would warn Sauruv on the phone that the chemo was over and we were heading home so that they would have time to tidy up our guest room and go back to their quarters. Now that Jagdish was under Sunita's influence, she had forbidden him to take part in such deception and hence the animosity that had sprung up between Jagdish and Sauruv.

Now that chemo was over and MS felt fit enough to drive, a driver was redundant. It was that much more money going down the drain, so Jagdish had been given a month's notice to find a new job. We had no inkling of his desperate desire to stay put on account of Sunita. The notice to leave our services and Sunita's reluctance to marry him made an overwrought Jagdish slit his wrist in my nursing home. There was an awful lot of blood in the kitchen, bloody shoe prints in the lounge and drops of blood on the landing and driveway, but no evidence of Jagdish. We were going for a wedding but I worried about him. What if he fainted on the way home or needed stitches? After repeated calls, his mother picked up the phone. I asked about him and he snatched the phone from her and snarled, 'You have thrown me out, that too around Diwali. I have done this because of you.'

I was shocked. What had I done to deserve such false accusations? I had taken his side all along against my husband. Now too I was doing MS's dirty work and tried to pacify Jagdish by assuring him of a Diwali gift and a sari for his mother and his bride when they found one. I also reminded him that we had given him ample notice.

24.10.13

Jagdish rang up to apologise when Sunita told him how hurt I was by his behaviour but it did not pacify me. Was it my fault that Sunita was not willing to have him and his mother was marrying him off to another? Why was he taking out his frustration on someone who had always been kind to him? He certainly was not a nice person to know, leave alone marry; Sunita was doing the right thing. Threatening to commit suicide so easily spoke of an unstable personality, a quality certainly not needed in a husband.

31.11.13

We went to Bengaluru for six days and had a very nice time, though, sadly, we had to ask Mona to put a mackintosh on MS's bed lest he leak through his diaper. Jessy became very attached to his grandfather. I was happy to see them make the most of the time we had to nurture this relationship. However brief, we enjoyed his company. I committed to memory his wonder at the white moon against a blushing sky, with homing birds, the way he flicked his head to remove the strand of jet-black hair that fell on one eye, the games we played on the terrace.

We also caught up with Amrit in Bengaluru, who tried to hide her shock on seeing MS's wasted form, his clothes dangling as if on a hanger. We went with her to the Mysore Silk Store to buy the famed south Indian silk saris. I stayed away from the bright red-pink-maroons that I usually wore. When Amrit insisted, I told her sadly that I did not know for how long I would be able to wear them. However, I bought an elegant black crepe sari with grey embroidery and two crinkly chiffons, parrot green and dark grey with a thin gold border. Of these two, Amrit gifted me one and forced MS to buy the other as a belated Karva Chauth present, while I paid for the most expensive black crepe.

5.11.13

Our wonderful Bengaluru visit over, we set off early for the airport to avoid the evening rush. The flight that was scheduled for 7.30 p.m. eventually took off at 9.15 p.m. We decided to have coffee outside the airport, hoping it would be cheaper but Café Coffee Day was expensive and MS had us drag the luggage a long way searching for cheaper options.

'Why can't we have something decent for a change,' I grumbled.

Finally, we settled down for tea but MS took such a long time getting out the accompaniments, crisp chakli that Simar gave us, that the tea turned cold. I lost patience and gave him a piece of my mind. We quarrelled over my having no patience (which was true, given his weakened condition) and time flew in a jiffy. Back at Delhi airport MS was efficiency personified. He got down the heavy luggage from the carousel and booked the prepaid taxi, chores that I would have to learn to do myself later.

We visited Bengaluru once again for Jessy's first birthday. Though we had a wonderful time, MS's miserliness was the talk of the town. He would not pick up a phone fearing he would have to pay roaming charges and contributed only twenty thousand rupees out of the one lakh we had decided to give our only grandchild on his first birthday. He made Simar pay our taxi fare, which was fair enough as Simar was a son and barely did anything for us, but when he made Amrit pay the auto fare to her house, it was the limit. I forced him to give her the money later. The grateful glance she directed towards me said it all.

While returning to Delhi from Jessy's birthday celebrations, there was dense winter fog. The plane ride was as bumpy as it goes with the wings dipping left then right and we feared the worst. Ruby, who had accompanied us, held on to my hand for dear life. Planes were being diverted to warmer climes but the airports at Jaipur, Ahmedabad were already full and we ended up in Nagpur! The two hours within the narrow confines of the cramped seat gave me severe back strain.

MS and Ruby got up so that I could lie down for a while to stretch my aching back. Ruby's family rang up repeatedly, so did Paramjit, but not a call from my son or daughter-in-law though I had informed them of our precarious situation. Neither enquired whether we had reached safely or not. With a sick feeling I realised that they did not care whether we lived or died.

I revisited my cancer diary after a long time. Let's hope it always remains that way. The five-year survival rate was about 20 per cent in stage IV bladder cancer. I hoped and prayed that MS was among the 20 per cent survivors, but if he wasn't, I prayed that he did not suffer. It will soon be a year since the diagnosis and though we have been through a lot, he has always maintained an attitude of normalcy. Denial was the protective mechanism he had subconsciously adopted to cope with the situation. It was not for me to burst his bubble. The grudges I bore against MS had dissolved in tears and I tried not to let the stains of our past smudge our present. Living together for forty years is a great deal of togetherness, though it was more for the worse than for the better. We had become habituated to each other and our habits were stronger than ever.

These days, I even discovered in him qualities that I have learnt to admire – the courage with which he has faced his dreadful disease, the way he continued to live as if nothing untoward had happened. He even took to life in diapers in his stride and would blithely take some along to his clinic to change in between patients. I wondered if I would have had the courage to carry on thus with my life had I been in his place. Being so vociferous about his many faults, I decided to voice my appreciation while he was still alive. No point enumerating them to others when he was dead and gone, and risk being laughed at. In a rare show of affection, I hugged him from behind as he reached up to get something and said, 'Good or bad, you are all I've got,' which melted his heart a wee bit.

Then I told him, 'There are things about you that I have learned to admire over the last year or so.'

'What?' he asked, surprised.

'You have never let the disease get the better of you. No complaining, no whining, no begging for pity.'

At this he held my hand and intertwining his fingers with mine said with feeling, 'You are my biggest asset.'

It was the first heartfelt compliment he had paid me in almost forty years of married life, that is, if I decided to take it as a compliment. It could also mean that he had taken the right decision in keeping me chained to morbid matrimony despite my desperation to leave, for I was serving him well now. There I go again, harping on my magnanimity (though not aloud) which negated any good that I have done.

He never complained about the lack of interest by our children, perhaps because I was there for him. I was the one who felt forsaken. Neither son rang up to find out about the result of MS's three-monthly follow-up visits. Overwhelmed by their neglect, I rang up Simar and said, '*Lawaris chod diya hai humko* (You have abandoned us).'

As for Karan, I dared not tell him how his indifference hurt, for he would mouth words that would make me writhe in agony for days.

8.1.14

MS has gone for tests. He will have to take the reports along with him for his follow-up visit tomorrow. He wanted me to come along but I had a caesarean section to perform and he did not need someone to hold his hand for an ultrasound or a blood test. I had been through worse without his support.

Though I appeared outwardly calm, the stress manifested as an attack of migraine. The one thing good about ageing was the decrease in the frequency of migraine attacks. They had returned with a vengeance along with his cancer. The ultrasound took an inordinately long time. He was mighty pleased to learn that the capacity of his ileal bladder was 900, which was actually not good. The doctor asked MS to evacuate his bladder frequently even if he did not feel the urge, so that bacteria didn't grow in the stagnated urine.

21.1.14

MS wet his bed after a long while. I never held such accidents against him, as I did his atrocious toilet manners; the latter were voluntary acts of omission while he had no control over this. After exerting himself at the clinic, it was well-nigh impossible to set an alarm and wake up every three hours to change his diaper, but getting up in the middle of the night to help him sponge his back, and changing his clothes and bed sheets was worse, for I was not getting younger myself and I got a severe backache.

Though I did not actually play nursemaid most of the time, I woke up whenever he got up to use the washroom and could only sleep after he returned. Today, on finding his sheet drenched in the morning, the smartass quietly covered it with his quilt and left for work, leaving behind that much extra work for us! It wasn't as if it would not be discovered. The servant recoiled at the sight, so I changed his bed sheet, quilt and pillow covers and gave him a piece of my mind when he returned from work. Washing and drying a urine-wet quilt was unnecessary extra work. Thankfully, the new sweeper, Ganga, was a helpful soul and did not grumble when he had to wash the huge mound of soiled linen.

My hospital organised a free health check-up for the doctors and their families. With various wires attached to my chest that recorded my heart tracings continuously, I exercised on the treadmill. The ECG showed negative changes, which meant that my treadmill test was positive. I would need an angiography and perhaps a stent or two, even a bypass, if there was blockage in my coronary arteries. This was cause for worry.

I, who shooed away relatives crowding around a patient's bed, had no relatives to stand by me if I needed hospitalisation! The children lived far away, Ruby would be leaving for the US in a few days and MS I knew would sleep by me only at night for he had not missed his clinic even for the birth of his first son. On learning of my predicament, the cardiologist suggested that I go for a stress thallium test, which would show a blockage. This would mean I did not have to get it treated immediately and could get it done later, when Simar got leave.

2.4.14

My stress thallium test was scheduled for today and I had specifically asked the stopgap help Ramesh (Sauruv was on leave) not to rub me the wrong way as he usually did. He forgot to pack my breakfast and berated me for giving him so much work that he did not have the time. This led to an altercation, which caused palpitations, breathlessness and high BP at a time I specifically wanted to avoid it. Every so often, I have seen that if you expose your vulnerability to anyone, they poke needles into it. Though the extra work on account of MS's illness made Sauruv throw a fit at times (despite a handsome increase in pay), he was essentially a neat and efficient worker. Ramesh had nothing to redeem him. Slow and inefficient, he would threaten to leave with the ominous words '*Mera hisaab kar do* (Clear my account)'. The cheek! I had recently saved him almost a lakh of rupees. His brother had sustained a head injury after falling down a flight of stairs. Blood poured out of his ear, which the neurosurgeon, a colleague (whom I begged to treat him for free), said was a good thing, as it would not collect inside and compress the brain. She took the risk of treating him at home provided they agreed to get him admitted if he lost consciousness or had fits. Thankfully, that did not happen and the man recovered completely. And this was how Ramesh was repaying my kindness when my turn came. At times such as these I recalled Mother Teresa's words which gave me solace:

> The good you do today may be forgotten tomorrow, do good anyway …
> For you see, in the end, it is between you and God,
> It was never between you and them anyway.

Empty stomach, we went to the nuclear medicine department of the diagnostic centre nearby, which belonged to good Dr Pankaj who had done MS's first ultrasound. They inserted an IV cannula in a vein on the back of my hand, which hurt as I held the handles of the treadmill. While the exercising was at its peak, they injected the thallium and told me to go home and return after one and a half hours for the nuclear films. Ruby's husband was to drop her at the centre to be with me when MS left for his clinic, as we knew he would. I had brought my car along to drive myself home after the procedure. What I did not know was that I had to drive back in the middle of the procedure too with the venflon in the back of my hand. It hurt badly when I had to curl my fingers around the steering wheel. Back to the centre I drove again, this time with Ruby, who replaced my uncaring husband. They took films, injected some more thallium and made me wait for a couple of hours to see the perfusion in its resting state. Ruby and I sat in their waiting room and gossiped.

I was given a McDonald's burger that Ruby did not share as she was fasting, which was good because the meal was not a mere courtesy, but a fatty meal I had to have before the next set of images.

Once again Dr Pankaj did not charge me a rupee. He showed an avid interest in my recently published book. Ruby punctured my elation by sagaciously stating that she did not read it nor did my other siblings, indirectly denouncing my book as porn, written by the black sheep of the family. To be published by a reputed publisher was the culmination of years of solitary struggle as a writer and my sister publicly dissociated herself from anything she thought would tarnish the family name. Not knowing what to make of the turn our conversation had taken, Dr Pankaj quickly asked, 'What does your husband say about the book?'

To shock the good doctor further, I declared, 'MS does not read either, so he does not know what is in the book!'

The poor fellow took a while to recover and added lamely, 'It's your own life and so what if you have had an affair.'

The report showed a normal perfusion and an ejection fraction of 70 per cent, so no stenting was needed. Thank heavens for that. Now all that remained were MS's tests and if they were fine I expressed a wish to take a small vacation on our fortieth anniversary. We deserved the break. That two incompatible people had managed to live together for forty years without killing each other was cause enough for celebration. Moreover, who knew when the sleeping cobra of cancer would strike again and a fiftieth anniversary seemed a highly unlikely event. By the way, once again both my sons let me down; neither rang up to find out the result of my stress thallium!

23.4.14
MS got his routine tests done. Blood sugar levels were high, his bones were weak but on the plus side his ultrasound showed lesser residual urine and chest X-ray showed no secondaries. All in all, it was a good result. He was cancer-free as of now, and as this coincided with our fortieth marriage anniversary it doubled the reason for celebrations. In my jubilation, I forgot that MS did not have it in him to enjoy life, even after this life-changing event.

3.5.14
His baraat had come to my door on this day forty years ago and all he got for me was a bloody gajra! I could cry with frustration. My dream of a weekend in the hills remained a dream. Paramjit was of marriageable age and with no father to arrange a match for him he had come to meet a prospective bride he had met on shaadi.com. He got a new ice-cream flavour for us to have at midnight to celebrate our anniversary but MS was too sleepy and I was too disappointed to stay awake till midnight, so we ate it before going to bed.

4.5.14
The three of us went by metro to Sheesh Ganj Gurdwara in Chandni Chowk to meet the girl from Meerut. As luck would have it, Paramjit's pants tore as he bent to tie his shoelaces. He rushed to a readymade shop to get a new one before the girl arrived with her family. She was slim, fair and pretty like her mother. Her father and brother had clipped their beard. Paramjit had not trimmed his, though it should not matter much for my sons had cut off their hair. We interacted with them for about an hour. They parted with the words 'We will come to Nainital' which boded well.

After this, we went to Daryaganj by e-rickshaw to the famous Sunday pavement book bazaar to browse the second-hand books. I loved the feel and smell of old books and made some nice buys. I could see that the other two, not so enamoured of books, were bored. We had lemon soda from a wayside cart, which I knew I should not on account of my IBS, but the heat was killing. Soon we were headed back to Chandni Chowk amid a mad rush of smoke-belching traffic for dahi bhalle and tikki at the famed Natraj, which again boded ill for my stomach, but I had come here after ages and would not miss them for anything. I also bought a lavender chikankari sari and some kurtas from my own money and enjoyed our anniversary, no thanks to MS. I had worn a gajra in my hair but the sweet smell of jasmine only served to whet my anger against him.

Paramjit left in the evening and depression took hold of me. I told MS that I was deeply disappointed. 'Who knows if we will see our fiftieth anniversary,' I lamented. I wasn't even sure of our next but did not say so.

'We will,' he said, just to shut me up.

'In the highly unlikely event that both of us will be alive then, what difference would it make?' He kept quiet. 'We could have gone out of station for the weekend. I had wanted to do so all along and had told you so a month in advance.'

Over the years, I had learnt the hard way never to expect anything from this man. This mantra had helped me survive this farce of a marriage but people do change for the better in changed circumstances. While he remained the hard-hearted, selfish, horrible man he always was, I had foolishly begun to expect again. I thought that a token of thanks was in order perhaps because I had invested so much in him during his illness. Besides the gajra, a dinner of tandoori chicken and dal makhni, plus a mango each, completed our fortieth anniversary celebrations – his way.

Much water had flowed under the bridge during the forty years with MS. As for life with Rajan, a tributary that ran parallel to the turbulent river of matrimony, it had been in spate during the monsoons of my departing youth, but now, a liaison gone sour was reduced to a mere trickle like the Yamuna in summer, revealing the dregs like rotting fish and plastic bottles. From these very bottles we had drunk the heady concoction of lust, love, guilt and fear. Now that the passion had waned, the negative traits accumulated, leading to further stagnation and decay. The extramarital attachment hung useless as an extra finger that I had yet not mustered the courage to amputate.

25.4.14

Rajan had more or less faded from my life and I couldn't care less. So I was surprised to receive a distraught phone call where he blabbered incoherently between sobs. I asked him to calm down, to drink a glass of water and begin again. It turned out that he had opened their bank locker and found it empty. His wife, Sneh, was stunned when she heard the news as her jewellery was kept there too. Accusations were flung to and fro, for only Rajan and his daughter-in-law had access to the locker key and she had opened it a few days earlier. His wife watched them quarrel with glazed eyes not saying a word – because she couldn't! Her blood pressure had escalated to such an alarming degree that it burst an artery in her brain. Only when her nose began to drip blood did the warring parties notice her.

A CT scan revealed brain haemorrhage, and she was instantly shifted to the operation theatre. Her skull was sawed open and a piece of bone as large as her palm was removed so that blood from the ruptured blood vessel could flow out instead of compressing the brain. The bone thus removed was kept in her abdominal wall till she was well enough to have it put back in place. Quite like the Nobel laureate Malala who had been shot in the head at close range by the Taliban for propagating the education of the girl child. Though Malala's immediate surgery was performed in Pakistan, further treatment was carried out in Birmingham, England. However, they never replaced the bone ensconced in her abdomen, fearing it would infect the brain as the operation was done in haste in Pakistan and they weren't sure that all safety measures had been taken. Malala would always remain 'soft in the head' – at least in a part of it!

Despite immediate surgery, Sneh was to remain paralysed for life. Unlike cancer, which eventually kills, paralysis though debilitating was not life-threatening. Money flowed like water. She remained in the ICU for three months. The various tubes inserted in her body were removed one by one; only the gastric tube for oral alimentation remained. All she needed now was physiotherapy and nursing care, which could be done at home.

Sneh had three nurses who tended to her round the clock. She was visited by a physiotherapist and a speech specialist every day. Rajan sent me a picture of Sneh on a wheelchair as she was being discharged from the hospital. It horrified me. A new growth of grey hair bristled on her bald pate as her head had been shaved before surgery. A Ryle's tube protruded from her left nostril, which made it look bigger than the right one and crooked. She had dark shadows under her glazed eyes that stared unseeingly out of her gaunt face. She was totally paralysed on the left side and was unable to speak.

Besides the humongous hospital fees, the nurses cost him thirty thousand a month plus boarding and lodging. Moreover, the daughter-in-law accused him of stealing her jewellery and wanted it back or an equivalent price for it. Her father, a police officer, and her brother ganged up against him while his adopted son, Sonu, stood by quietly, unable to meet his father's eye. Rajan desperately wanted Sneh to speak again to glean the truth. He would have to wait a long time, if not forever, for that to happen. Meanwhile he was utterly stressed out by the turn of events and the financial burden. As if this was not enough for the temperamental Rajan, his mother fell down the stairs and ended up with a compound fracture. She needed surgery and stitches. His home was converted into a veritable hospital.

All this made me wonder why God in His wisdom had punished our partners when the two of us were the 'culprits', at least in the eyes of society. Whatever the provocation, we had wronged our spouses. Why, then, did they suffer terrible diseases such as stroke and cancer? Maybe it was our punishment; maybe that was the cross we would bear till the end of time – theirs or ours.

In the unforeseen future, MS would expire late next year, Rajan's son would die of hepatic coma three years later, while his mother, unable to bear the loss of her only grandchild, would die of a massive heart attack two months after his death. All this while Sneh would watch, endure and grieve in silence. She would live for over ten years in this state before she succumbed to pneumonia. As for Rajan and me, we would continue as before: estranged, apart, alone.

24.7.14

Each time the electricity bill arrives, my heart sinks as I brace myself for a tirade from MS. It was as if I consumed the entire electricity at home. What a relief it will be for him if I died before him. No one would switch on the AC at home or in his car; no one would eat rice or onions; he would not have to hide fruit from anyone. No one would nag him. No one would embarrass him by whistling when happy, jumping into a heap of crisp autumn leaves with Choco for the sheer joy of it or getting drenched in the rain and, most important of all, there would be no one to write of things that any right-thinking person would carry to the grave. If only I'd had the good fortune to 'marry someone who enjoys your madness and not the idiot who forces you to be normal'.

I had wanted to marry a classmate who had the capacity to enjoy life as much as I did but my parents were against the match because he belonged to another religion. As if that mattered; compatibility was the most important thing in a marriage, but they did not seem to think so. According to my mother, what was there to dislike in MS. He was a good 'boy' who did not drink, gamble (not any more) or womanise. 'Not even with his wife,' I wanted to add but kept quiet, for it did not matter; I never got any joy from our union. I had stopped having sex with MS after I became intimate with Rajan – a serial monogamist, so to say. Now those days too were over but I never returned to MS that way again.

It again struck me that despite his pathological stinginess, his lack of concern for my welfare, his atrocious toilet manners, his halitosis, his squeezed-lemon sour expression when I wanted something from him his 'bechara' look when I irritated him, I wanted him around. For better or worse, he was all I had. As they say, 'If you don't get what you like, learn to like what you have'.

It was comforting to share my table, my home with another human during my twilight years. The routine of our lives depended upon his timetable; I depended upon him to take me to social events and the cinema hall, for I had never gone to such places alone. At these scant strings that bound us, I clutched. I had become habituated to him and hearts are easier to break than habits.

28.7.14

Rising above rancour and regrets, I tried to make life as pleasant as I could for him but all the goodwill I had generated towards him came crashing down yesterday. I was unwell and took a paracetamol tablet before going to bed. I also told MS to make sure that the help did not wake me up early as I would not be able to go for a swim. He 'forgot'. Maybe he did. I gave him the benefit of doubt. And then he switched off the AC before he went for his morning walk. Drenched in sweat, vulnerable and weak, I lay there staring at the ceiling. How cruel could a person be to grudge a sick person a few hours of restful sleep to save a few rupees on electricity? I had adjusted and compromised all my life, but enough was enough.

No one else seemed to get the point. Like the time, desperate for a vacation, I asked a friend who was an avid traveller to suggest some place that did not cost a lot of money as my husband did not like to spend much. At this, she had retorted, '*Phir tu kharch* (Then you spend).' Besides our separate bills, any large expense that cropped up was shared equally between us and I had been talking only about his half of the share.

While I was given to flashes of anger – bubbles that subsided as soon as they frothed over – MS was more subtle. It took so little for him to do what any decent person would but he chose not to. For instance, lifting the toilet seat before peeing. Though his habit had not changed, my physiology had altered with the passage of years. One of the consequences of menopause was incontinence. I could barely hold my urine long enough to reach the washroom, and if I spent a disgusting extra minute cleaning the seat with tissue paper before plonking on it, I would end up wetting my clothes with his urine and mine. I threatened to pee on his clothes purposely to let him know how it felt, but it made no difference. He knew I would not stoop so low. Now that the children (for whom I had put my life on hold) had grown up and gone, had it not been for his cancer, I would have left him for the mental torture he inflicted and the physical repugnance he evoked.

19.8.14

This year his chemo doctor had suggested CECT of the abdomen with pelvis and thorax instead of a PET. MS took the appointment for 6.30 a.m. so that he could reach his clinic in time. He also wanted me to go separately in my own car so that he was saved the time and effort of driving me home.

As MS had to spend the first hour and a half drinking the contrast fluid before the CECT and getting up early made me cranky, I decided to go an hour later with our breakfast. I reached just before he was to enter the claustrophobic chamber. Clumsy with panic, he removed his ring, watch and cell phone and handed them to me. I wished him luck and sat in the waiting area with the relatives of other patients. He returned after an hour and gave his urine sample for cytology. We were asked to wait for another half hour to watch out for drug reaction due to the dye. In the meantime, we had breakfast, with coffee bought from the stall downstairs. His need for me over, he reverted to his original self, insisting that I gulp the coffee quickly as he was getting late. He dared not leave me to finish it alone in peace (after all, I had come in my own car) for he would never hear the end of it. I burnt my tongue in the haste.

20.6.14

Amrit rang up to enquire about MS's report. It smote me afresh that her love for her brother was unconditional. Even I needed him around for selfish reasons. Once again, neither of the children rang up to find out about the CECT result. Whatever my issues with MS, I could not bear the fact that his children were so unconcerned; it boded ill for my future too. If not affection, at least on account of a sense of duty they should have kept in touch. He was their father, a father they (especially Karan) thought I had wronged. During those turbulent years, his sympathies lay with Papa. Why then was he so unconcerned? Neither had bothered to ask about my stress thallium result too, which had pained me. Why is it that the very children we raise with such love, for whom we could lay down our lives, become so indifferent to our needs when they no longer need us? Karan would fleetingly broach the subject of making us US citizens then quickly retract his statement, saying that it was a tedious process that could take up to ten years.

22.8.14

Simar did not get the job satisfaction he craved in the much-hyped job in Bengaluru. Lack of basic equipment in an international hotel chain of repute irked and in a fit of pique he told his boss, 'I cannot work with you!' and got the answer that such a statement warranted.

'So when are you leaving?'

As I succinctly put it, '*Headmaster ko thappad maar aaya* (You have slapped the headmaster)! Now what?'

Jobs for chefs of his seniority were hard to come by. Most well-paying offers he got were from the Gulf, but as there were restrictions imposed on women in countries like Saudi Arabia, his wife, understandably, was not keen on going. He was under considerable stress, which added to my stress overload.

Though I worried about him and prayed for him, I was hurt that he had not bothered to ask about MS's results and told him so. Instead of being contrite he said, '*Main Mona ki birthday bhi bhool jaata hoon – voh hints deti rehti hai* (I forget Mona's birthday too though she keeps giving hints).' As if the two situations were the same.

This world functions purely on demand and supply, I reflected sadly. The situation was different with Simar's in-laws, for they were in demand. Being a non-working couple, they looked after Jessy when the two went to work. He was all over his mother-in-law when she had an abnormal TMT, though he did not bother to ask about my stress thallium report. Now that his in-laws were going away for two weeks, we were wanted in Bengaluru to babysit. The least he could do was confirm that his father was fit enough to travel before he booked our tickets, but that was too much to expect.

To paraphrase Ruth Westheimer, 'Our way is not soft grass, it's a mountain path with lots of rocks that hurtles down toward death.'

The serpent has struck again! The cancer returned with a vengeance, forcing me to restart my cancer diary – a diary that not even my worst enemy should ever be obliged to write. In the intervening time, we/he forgot that he was a 'cancer survivor' – one who triumphantly walks out of the ominous valley to die of other causes years later. I wonder what a cancer survivor with recurrence is called – a 'cancer reviver'? Why does the nomenclature offend me so much? What difference will it make?

During the interim period MS had learnt nothing from his brush with death. There was no gratitude to the heavens above for the fresh lease of life. There did not arise in him a desire to live every moment to the fullest, to fulfil wishes that had been hitherto postponed, to be kind and considerate to his mate. Most surprising of all, he never thought of setting his affairs in order, telling me about his assets or making a will.

In fact, MS appeared so normal that, I am ashamed to admit, I began to suspect the diagnosis! Stage IV bladder carcinoma was supposed to progress rapidly and had a very poor five-year survival rate. He developed diabetes, and though he bought a glucometer to test his blood sugar levels, he did it surreptitiously lest I ask him to test mine too. The one time he did test my sugar, I was aghast to learn that he had sunk to pathological depths of parsimony. He had used the same needle he had pricked his own finger with. Thank God he was not HIV positive, though I am not too sure that research has ever been done on this mode of cancer spread.

5.8.15
MS began to have pain in his abdomen at night, for which he self-medicated with tablets and even asked me to give him an injection one night. He thought it was due to the large incisional hernia he had developed after cancer surgery but as the gap was so wide there was no question of intestinal strangulation. He also experienced loss of appetite and fatigue. There was weight loss and weakness that forced him to lie down, though he made a feeble attempt to go for his morning walk. He did not even bother to read the newspaper, an essential part of his daily routine. It lay tightly rolled in its black rubber band, accusingly virginal. Fear began to gnaw at my innards, so I confided in Dr Verma. He ordered a CECT. We reached at 9 a.m. on the appointed day. The radiologist, a tall, slim woman on pointy black high heels, told us that MS would have to drink the non-ionic contrast for two hours instead of the usual one and a half hours on account of his hernia. So it was a glass of the solution every 20 minutes.

While he did so in the waiting room, I wrote a chapter of my new book on my computer. I also befriended the radiology technician, a handsome fellow named Thomas. After the procedure, he gave me some ominous news: there was perhaps a lesion in the liver, which he wanted me to confirm with the doctor. I approached her with a palpitating heart, but she suggested that I let her go over the films thoroughly before she gave her opinion. As MS had had enough for the day in his fragile state, I did not tell him what they suspected. Time enough to learn about it later. Yama came riding on his buffalo in a swirl of dust to take MS away and I was no Sati Savitri who would challenge the god of death for my husband.

6.8.15

MS rang up from his clinic in the afternoon to tell me that he felt giddy. He had taken two teaspoons of glucose in water suspecting hypoglycaemia, but on testing, his blood sugar was 235 mgms! As he was not up to driving back home, he had decided to rest at a neighbour's place. I told Paramjit (who had come from Nainital on business) to go to the clinic in an auto, pick up MS and drive him back home. En route they could stop at the hospital to collect the CECT report. I insisted that he go inside along with his uncle to collect it, for I did not want MS to read it alone. However, it made sense to get the opinion of his medical oncologist before coming home. Dr Verma took his time over lunch and other patients, and could attend to MS only a good two and a half hours later. Meanwhile, Paramjit read out the report to me on the phone. The disease had spread to MS's liver, lymph nodes and the adrenal gland. I was devastated and could only imagine MS's state of mind. The weather seemed to match our mood, for after days of dryness, the skies darkened with clouds of impending doom. Lightning danced through my heart while thunder resounded like a death knell. It began to pour. 'Who'll comfort the comforter?'

To my astonishment, it was Choco who did it. The thunder so frightened him that for the first time in his life he pushed open the door himself and ran to me for comfort. I scooped him into my arms and held him to my breast, as much comforted by the warm, furry body as he was by my presence.

MS was shell-shocked. I consoled him by mouthing words that sounded hollow to my own ears. 'We will fight it out together, like we did last time,' I said, though I knew that with metastatic cancer, he would never get well. But hope was what he wanted, for hope conquers all.

Once again, I had to take the decisions for his treatment. The doctor had wanted us to get MS admitted immediately for PET and FNAC of the liver and give him the first dose of second-generation chemo. As this meant a hospital stay of three days, we decided to get the liver biopsy from the OPD.

His blood sugar came down to 98 that night and he celebrated it by eating an entire piece of barfi. God knows how many days he had left to enjoy the little pleasures of life. Years later, during the COVID-19 pandemic, people were advised to enjoy the leisure of lockdown, the forced togetherness instead of giving in to claustrophobia and depression. Well, I had learnt that lesson during these days and could cope very well with the forced seclusion.

Despite my best intentions, we had petty quarrels over trivialities like which show to watch on TV. The worst quarrel we had was over his blood sugar testing. Asking me to prick his finger, MS handed me the needle in such a way that it pricked my hand and drew blood. Once again, to my horror, I learnt that he was using a disposable needle over and over again.

7.8.15

MS woke me up at 4 a.m. as his usual home remedies brought little relief from his abdomen pain. It was due to the stretch of his liver capsule that had enlarged with metastatic cancer and it would only get worse with time; of course, I did not tell him that. I gave him an Ultracet tablet and after a while he slept while I lay awake, thinking of the days and months I would watch him suffer and shrink into a bundle of bones contained in a loose bag of skin. My shoulders sagged at the thought of endless futile nursing care and of the fear of living alone. I longed to buckle under and let fatigue take me down with MS, but I was destined to live so that I could serve MS till his dying day. But as I heard a man telling the wife of a cancer patient in a TV serial, 'Being a rock takes all you got.'

Mona had got her parents covered in her company insurance, and when her father needed a by pass, they hardly had to spend anything on him. Thankfully, this had prompted Simar to do the same for us. It would now come in useful, for we had exhausted our resources. I told him to send the card details, if he could not come himself. We were in dire need of moral support but he had more important things to do – attend his wife's nephew's first birthday in Bengaluru, for which their tickets from Mumbai were already booked. Instead of commiserating, Mona asked us not to tell Amrit about the secondaries now, as she would cry and spoil the party. I managed not to utter a word of admonishment.

A colleague, Nita, who was a member of the Brahma Kumaris, had arranged for a group of doctors to go to Mount Abu to witness luminaries like Sister Shivani speak and perhaps redeem our souls. I thought it was a good idea and had paid for the train tickets before we learnt of the recurrence of MS's cancer. In the changed circumstances, I realised it would be foolish to go. How could we attend the meditation sessions in this state? Tactfully, Nita told me that there was no hurry as the tickets could be cancelled at the last moment too. Moreover, four cancer specialists were going along, and in the Brahma Kumari centre at Mount Abu they had a holistic hospital. She listed the pros one by one. The place was full of positive vibes. Her father-in-law's lung condition had improved dramatically here. We didn't have to go to the hall but could listen to the sessions from our room as there were loudspeakers everywhere. Someone could bring food for us so that we did not have to go to the dining room. This made me decide in favour of going, for I doubted if we would ever go for a holiday together again, that too at such a salubrious, holy place like Mount Abu, but painful nights like the last one forced me to rethink.

9.8.15

On Sunday MS went with Paramjit to the diabetologist for his fluctuating blood sugar levels. He was put on insulin, which he had to inject subcutaneously in his abdomen. Though the insulin pen made it almost painless, it was another setback, for he seemed to take his diabetes more seriously than his cancer. After the consult, they went to Gurdwara Nanak Piao and later to the mechanic to get MS's precious car serviced. Paramjit spent an entire day attending to his uncle's needs.

Having an entire Sunday to myself after ages was a luxury that I intended to make full use of. Uninterrupted, I typed chapters of the book for nurses I had been commissioned to write. After I got tired, I packed for our trip to Mount Abu and the physicality of the act distracted me. In the evening I went for a leisurely swim, and as there was no hurry to return to an empty house, I relaxed on the deckchair by the pool, watching twilight smear the skies and darken the green crowns of trees. Egrets winged their way home in a V formation while a solitary one lagged behind.

I watched Gulzar on TV and remembered seeing him twice in person and shaking his soft hand once. To think that he had started life as a mechanic! Though the calloused hands of a car mechanic would have been more 'manly', the world would never have known the jewels mined from his mind – words that gave so much joy. As of now, he was saying that happy moments were momentary, like sparklers, while sorrow was an incense stick that burns slowly and leaves its fragrance for long after.

17.8.15

Each year the Brahma Kumaris held a three-day session to heal the healers. It was meant to make us spiritually strong, for ours was one of the most stressful professions in the world. Over fourteen hundred doctors had come from all over India and abroad to take a slice of peace back with them. The train journey by night towards Mount Abu was comfortable enough. However, the road up the hill was blocked by a landslide that was still being cleared. So we stayed at the bigger centre at the foot of Mount Abu. The implication of secondaries struck me like a stone at Abu Road railway station. As we got down from the train, I made MS carry the heavier piece of luggage. A kind oncologist rushed over to ease him of the burden and told me in an aside, 'Heavy weights can lead to pathological fractures of fragile bones in a cancer patient with metastasis!'

As promised, we were given a separate room. Pure saatvik food was served in the huge dining area where it was made with goodwill, along with the chanting of prayers. This was supposed to have a positive influence on one's health, as opposed to that made by the indifferent hands of a grumpy servant. We roamed about the campus, resting when MS felt the need to do so. I noticed that both men and women around the place mostly wore white. I had brought coloured clothes as they fare better on journeys and had to make do with them. Though I loved pastel shades, there arose in me a subconscious desire to wear bright colours as it would look improper to flaunt my reds and fuchsia pinks after ...

However, I did ask Nita why she hadn't told me that we were supposed to wear white. 'It's all right to wear what you want. There is no dress code; we do it of our own free will,' she said. That night as MS slept, I sat down with pen and paper to empty my heavy heart. Sorrow was a catalyst that converted unshed tears into words. Mulling over the colour white I wrote:

Virginal white or the white of widowhood – white was an asexual colour. Time enough to wear it for the rest of my life …

I befriended an oncologist from Apollo and discussed MS's case with him. He advised me not to subject MS to the second generation chemo as it would be more toxic and less effective. 'All he needs now is TLC – tender loving care.' This made me think. If I were the sufferer, I would have heeded his advice instantly, but I had to think twice where MS was concerned. For all his worldliness, he had a childlike faith in the ability of chemo to make him well again. Hope was all he had to sustain him and I was not going to take that from him.

18.8.15

After we returned, the doctors who had gone from Delhi to attend the retreat formed a WhatsApp group called 'Soulmates'. In this group I posted a note for Sister Shivani. It read:

> Today has been a difficult day for me; my heart was heavy. I thought of asking you to pray for us then felt ashamed of myself for this was not what you had taught us. You have shown me the way and I have to walk alone, so I shed negative emotions along with my tears and meditated for a while, after which I felt energised enough to take on the world, cancer kya cheez hai?

A doctor in our group sent me the following note:

> You are one of the liveliest persons I have met. You are a source of inspiration to anyone who comes in contact with you. The power within and the super power are both with you along with uncountable positive wishes.

Though it felt good to be appreciated thus, the one message I waited for (from Sister Shivani) did not arrive. It would have been a morale boost.

We reached ACH at 9 a.m. for MS's liver biopsy. The very thought of a needle piercing his abdomen had troubled MS the whole night. He got up at 4 a.m. and asked me to hold his hand. I did so and reassured him that it would be painless. Being a doctor, I was allowed inside. MS lay on the table facing the wall. He was given local anaesthesia and a lumbar needle was inserted into the suspicious area of his liver under ultrasound guidance. I was terrified to see it move up and down with each breath. What if it tore through his liver? Thankfully, he was asked to hold his breath, after which some blood and tissue were withdrawn with a syringe and spread on slides. Thank God for ultrasound guidance in modern times. During my internship days, liver biopsy was a blind procedure and once the needle pierced a major blood vessel in the liver, killing the poor patient. MS was kept under observation in the casualty for two hours.

As it was a prerequisite for the second-generation chemo, we had to get a cardiac echo done. As there was no free slot available here, I requested the cardiologist at my hospital to squeeze us in between his appointments. He graciously agreed. So I drove MS all the way there. By the time all this was over, I was exhausted and could only imagine the stress MS was under. The endurance he had to muster to actually go through it all!

Just when my confidence was at its lowest ebb, I got a message from Sister Shivani on our Soulmates WhatsApp group which lifted my spirits considerably. She wrote:

> Congratulations, doctor. You both are a source of inspiration for us. You are always protected under the canopy of Baba's love and blessings. All Soulmates will meditate for you daily. Collective consciousness will radiate powerful vibrations to both your beautiful souls. This karmic account shall soon be over.

True, 'this karmic account shall soon get over' even if it was settled with the currency of suffering and death, I thought.

19.8.15

I got up, deeply depressed. I had to send rakhis to my brothers abroad, a ceremonial yearly reminder for their protection in times of need. But except for the initial call after the diagnosis, they did not ring me up again – neither to ask how we were coping nor to reassure me of their support. Though Ruby lived in Delhi, she could not spare the time, embroiled as she was in litigation and the care of her grandchildren. As for our children, they carried on with their own lives, unconcerned with the chaos in ours. I longed for comforting arms to hold me while I gave vent to my grief, but there was no one in this whole world who could offer solace. With a heavy heart and heavy step, I went with MS to ACH for his PET scan. As the CT abdomen was positive, it was important to know if there were secondaries elsewhere in the body. As usual, I shed the heaviness in my heart with a few tears, a few words.

The 'few words' that despondency spawned, I posted on Soulmates.

of all his accounts, though I knew they were vastly depleted on account of the shop he had recently bought. The last thing I wanted was a showdown with our sons for his assets. As this did not entail transferring his earnings in my name during his lifetime, he initiated the process. I also asked him to will the shop in my name, but on this I had pushed my luck too far. He looked at me as a goat would at a butcher, so I let it pass. I knew that my sons would not create any hassles in the succession but every parent thinks that, and animosity, legal battle, even murder over property do occur in families. It was only right that matters be put in black and white to avoid dispute.

Did MS continue to think that he was immortal and the secondaries were just another roadblock that I would help him overcome? The PET scan showed involvement of the lower lobe of the left kidney and part of the stomach besides the secondaries seen in the CECT. As for the biopsy, though the written report was not yet ready, his doctor had got verbal intimation from the lab, confirming malignancy, which was as expected. *'Jahan satyanaas wahan sava satyanaas'* I thought sadly for the prognosis would remain the same – bad. Despite the sad news, despite the pain in the abdomen and loss of appetite, MS went for his evening clinic. Maybe it was the incentive he needed to live.

21.8.15

I was surprised to find MS at home when I returned after a busy day at work. He really must be ill to forsake his clinic; that was the parameter by which I judged his wellness. The poor man was steadily wasting away. The thinned-out face beneath a huge skull pulled at my heartstrings. I held his hand and he did not let go. After a long while, he slept. Never in my life had I felt so helpless.

22.8.15

Today was the first day of MS's first chemo cycle after metastatic disease. For the first time Simar would be going with MS and the two would be staying overnight at the hospital as there could be drug toxicity and severe side effects. I met them in the afternoon after attending my OPD. The chemo had just started and MS had already wet his bed. He got up to change just when the doctor arrived for his rounds. Quickly I covered the wet patch with the blanket to cover his embarrassment.

Alone at home for the first night in my life, I envisaged such a future and a shiver went down my spine. Afraid of the very servant I usually ordered about, I had an early dinner and sent him packing. I tried to find solace by holding Choco to my breast but he grew impatient and wriggled out of my grasp. I got up with a blinding headache in the middle of the night and wondered if I had burst an artery.

23.8.15

I tidied up our room, removed objects that could gather dust, changed the curtains, to minimise the chance of MS catching infection and waited and waited. When they did not arrive at the expected time, I began to worry and rang up Simar to learn that the discharge was being delayed; first, due to the insurance paperwork and then because MS would get up to pass urine every so often that his drip had to be disconnected and reconnected repeatedly. His fragility made movement slow and all this took time. When they finally returned, MS appeared sick and exhausted, so I let him rest in our darkened room.

After settling him in, I went to the living room to meet my sister and her family. They had come to look up MS but I would not allow them in, as he could catch an infection. We

And soon I got replies like:

> Dear madam, we look upon you as a source of inspiration. God will definitely help you to come out of this difficult situation.

I answered:

> I consign negativity to paper so that positivity shines bright like a newly minted coin. Emptying my mind of depleting emotions through verse is my form of meditation. That is why all that is left is humour and positivity, and that is what I spread.

This was because I had made those in my compartment laugh their butts off during the train journey home from the Brahma Kumari centre.

The procedure over, we went upstairs. While I filled the pre-authorisation form (Simar's company insurance would take care of the cost this time), I sent MS to get something to eat. He brought only one sandwich and tea and began eating it himself. My eyes filled with tears of rage.

'It's three o'clock and I am a diabetic too; did it not occur to you to bring something for me?'

'I thought you had already had something,' he said lamely, knowing very well that I was too embarrassed to eat alone in a strange place.

Contrite, he bought a sandwich and coffee for me.

20.8.15

I was offered the post of a unit head at the bigger super-speciality branch of my hospital but I refused as I could not forsake my husband at this stage even for such a lucrative job offer. Instead I tentatively asked MS to make me a nominee ordered food from outside and ate the heavy stuff – makhni dal, butter chicken and naan, which MS so enjoyed but was not allowed now. However, he could not refrain from taking a small portion of each after they left.

24.8.15

As Simar was here for a few days, I made Sauruv keep an eye on MS and went with him to see the movie *Manjhi*: *The Mountain Man*, based on a true story about a man who cut a road across the heart of a mountain in twenty-two years with no help, so that his village folk could access medical aid in a mere four-kilometre journey. His ailing wife could not make the forty-four kilometres around the mountain and had died on the way.

After the movie, Simar dropped me at the gate and drove away for some errand. A horrible sight greeted my eyes. The toilet door was ajar and MS was standing by the sink, smeared in shit. Loose stools had slid down his underwear and pyjamas to pool on his slippers. Perhaps he had run out of toilet paper, for the toilet pot was clogged with shit-smeared newspaper. I had no idea why he was not wearing a diaper. There was a trail of loose stools from his bed to the toilet. He must have removed the soiled diaper the first time and not had the strength to wear another. He was passing stools every fifteen minutes (a terrible side effect of the new chemotherapy drugs) and Sauruv, who had been entrusted to look after him during the couple of hours we were away, was sitting in the other room watching TV. He had not the slightest inkling of what was going on here. Though I blamed myself for ditching MS at this stage, he did not utter a single word of reproach. He thought that I would scold him for the stinking mess he had left all over the place. I bathed him with warm water, removed the shit from between his toes, made him wear a diaper and fresh clothes, gave him the requisite medicine to control diarrhoea and put him to bed. After that I cleaned up the mess he had made. The room was cleaned with phenol and sprayed with a room freshener. After this, as I washed the shit from his clothes and slippers (no help would do so) I grumbled to myself.

Paramjit had come in the morning on a business trip. He came at least once a month to replenish stocks in his shop from the wholesale market in Sadar Bazaar. On seeing the toilet clogged with newspaper, he donned a pair of gloves and without a frown of disgust at the awful smell thrust his hand in and pulled out the offending newspapers.

26.8.15

My spirits reached an all-time low. Though the number of stools had decreased, they had literally squeezed him dry. I wondered at the futility of a therapy whose dangers exceeded those of the disease.

Was it worth it, I asked myself and of Amrit, who had come from Bengaluru for Rakhi. She burst out crying despite her show of bravado and her clarion call for 'positive thinking'.

I escaped to my hospital and began crying long and hard myself. The sound of loud laughter from the adjoining cabin jarred. No one sympathised. Except for a cursory enquiry once, the doctor didn't ask after my husband. The hospital ayah was the only one who was kind. Almost in tears herself, she got me water and kept the patients at bay till I had composed myself. I rang up a senior oncologist in my hospital for a second opinion. He said, 'Give me two minutes, I'll get back to you.' He never called back.

Desperate for advice, I rang up another doctor whose mother had cancer of the cervix and I asked him what to do. 'Do not stop the chemo,' he stated categorically and that was enough to give me strength to fight it out. Incidentally, his mother's cancer was diagnosed early. She is still alive and cancer-free after so many years.

Amrit chose her own way of deciding. She went to the gurdwara and returned with renewed faith, said the vaak (the first lines of the page of the Guru Granth Sahib when it is opened at random) was positive and we should continue the treatment. I told her that I too had reached the same decision, for the slimmest of chances was worth taking.

27.8.15

We decided to keep MS downstairs till he recovered from the side effects of chemo. It was decided that Paramjit would stay with MS during the night. He was a real blessing in these times.

Sometimes I'd cry for MS and sometimes I'd cry because of him. I could not bear to see him so sick and weak and I could not bear the fact that he did not trust me even at this stage. As the driver's pay was due, instead of handing me the keys, he tried to wobble up the stairs to get it from his almirah. Thankfully, Amrit caught him on the first step, brought him back and gave the money from her own purse. I felt utterly humiliated but refrained from creating a scene. He could not help his nature, and like a scorpion, knew not else but to sting.

With Amrit away visiting relatives and Paramjit running errands, I came downstairs to share a simple meal with MS. I sat on the low stool by his side and he on the bedside sofa and we ate our food in companionable silence. I had broken the roti into bits and put it in the gravy for him to spoon into his mouth. It gladdened my heart to see that his appetite had returned after days.

Paramjit slept on the settee by MS's bedside in the nursing home downstairs, while Amrit slept on his bed by my side.

There would soon come a day when I would have to lie alone on that huge double bed.

28.8.15

I cut MS's nails for the first time in my life, which made Amrit take pictures of this historical event with all of us laughing over the act. We had a simple lunch of pea pulao with curd and it was heartening to see MS ask for a second helping.

That night we got MS upstairs because he was much better but also for another startling reason: Sunita told me the other nurse, Sapna, had been luring Paramjit into her room for a quickie.

I told MS that it was good to have him by my side again and held his hand. I badly wanted to sleep but MS talked about matters of no consequence and would not stop. I let him ramble, for it was a refreshing change from his usual lack of communication.

29.8.15

Today we celebrated Rakhi with aplomb. I wore a red suit with matching accessories and flowers, while Amrit dressed in a becoming orange suit. MS wore the blue checked shirt she had brought for him. Paramjit took pictures as she tied the rakhi around her brother's wrist. We all laughed and joked, aware that this would be the last Rakhi for this pair.

31.8.15

MS dressed up for the school where he had been doing medical check-ups of children for years, but realised that he was not up to it. So he rang up the principal of the school, and for the first time since he had got the disease, he acknowledged its existence. After all, for how long could the ruse of a surgery for prostate hypertrophy be used. She told him to rest and said he was always welcome back when he was fit, though both knew he would never go back. His predicament and her graciousness brought tears to his eyes for their association went back a long way.

Before leaving for his clinic for the first time since his chemo, MS asked for some change. I told him to take it from the purse in which I had kept the money he had finally given me for household expenses, again a first in our forty-one years of marriage. The change of heart was at the insistence of his sister, for he had already drained my dwindling resources.

1.9.15

I took MS to the hospital. On opening my purse, and in spite of myself I was shocked to see that he had taken not only the change but all the money in it. I turned to Amrit and lamented, 'This is how he tortures me night and day. Don't get taken in by his "poor thing" look. The moment he gets better, he is back to his old ways, as if he will never need me again.'

The date for the next chemo fixed, I filled the insurance forms and we were free by 11.30 a.m. As Amrit would be leaving soon, I dropped MS home and took her shopping and let her have the mandatory gol guppas and chat papdi. I was sorry to see her leave. Even though she did it solely for her brother, she was a major support and I could do with her help, as there was none forthcoming from any other quarter.

2.9.15

Perhaps Amrit had spoken to him, for MS gave me a bundle of hundred-rupee notes. I decided to alter his diet in a way that was practical, unlike his sister who would give him so much at breakfast that he was unable to eat anything later. So it was almonds with green tea on getting up, as we had always had. Instead of milk and cereals, I also put in protein powder and fresh fruits like bananas, which did not go down well with him. So I switched over to stuffed paratha with a boiled egg and milk with protein powder as his appetite gradually returned. He had nourishing chicken soup at 11 a.m., fruits and a high protein lunch and dinner with either paneer or liver. As he went to the clinic only in the evenings, I gave him a flask of milk with protein powder to take along.

After tipping Sauruv handsomely, Amrit had instructed him to prepare fresh, nutritious meals for MS. He did so till she was in Delhi, but he became lax after she left. Instead of fresh soup every day, he would prepare it in bulk and warm a portion whenever needed. Though I noticed, I said nothing, for Amrit was taking care of that part on the phone even from Bengaluru.

But one day when I was about to tick him off, MS signalled me to keep quiet. Despite his insolence, Sauruv was very much needed. He bathed MS when he was too weak to bathe himself and helped with a hundred other things. I also left MS under his supervision when I went to work so that I could be informed immediately of any setback. As for Sapna, though she did not wrinkle her nose at the smell while pouring buckets of water in the toilet pot, as the flush had stopped working, she'd forget to give MS his medicines in time.

3.9.15

MS lay in bed next to me, while I wrote in my diary. After a while MS began fingering the fabric of his new pyjamas and admiring its texture.

'What do you think of this?' he asked.

'Cool, isn't it, just chill,' I said.

At this he remembered the sexy Katrina Kaif song, 'Just chill, chill, just chill' and began moving his shoulders in an attempt to dance while lying down. His incisional hernia, the size of a musk melon, swayed this way and that and we laughed till tears ran down our cheeks. The movement also induced him to let loose a series of farts. Our world had now begun to revolve around his bowel movements. As he had been lamenting earlier that he hadn't cleared his bowels this morning, I now said, 'Just as trumpets announce the arrival of a king, farts announce the arrival of shit.'

Our laughter threshold already lowered by his ludicrous lying-down dance, we burst into peals of laughter once again.

4.9.15

MS exasperated me beyond limits. He came home late because he had stopped at Shakurpur to buy vegetables for they were cheap there. Was he plain stupid or did he have a secret death wish?

5.9.15

Karan rang up from the US asking me to stop working and look after Papa; he would put money in my bank for the treatment. This was not a viable proposition because MS was still going to his clinic and did not need constant supervision. He had been as surprised as I to see MS survive so long after stage four disease. As Karan was a liver specialist, I asked him, 'How much time do you give him?'

'Max one year.'

'And then what?' I asked. 'My post won't be waiting for me when I want it back. It will be difficult to get another attachment at this age. I enjoy exercising my surgical skills, and it would be cruel to ask me to give it up when I can work. Moreover, I can spend freely on whatever I want with my own money and save for my future, ailments and all, instead of begging you or Simar for money, which may or may not be forthcoming. I have always been an independent working woman and am used to not being answerable to anyone regarding my expenditure.'

He had no answer to that, so I continued, 'What I really need is assistance in looking after Papa. As you cannot come, I asked Simar if he can get himself transferred to Delhi and stay with us.'

'You want him to change his job for one year?' Karan was incredulous.

'And you want me, a senior citizen, to do the running around alone?' I flared.

'No, no, I didn't mean that.' He tried to placate me but I had had enough.

6.9.15

Dr Nita, who had taken us to Mount Abu, was now holding a Brahma Kumari programme at her place and had invited us. We got up at 6 a.m. to reach there at 7.15 a.m. Sister Shivani spoke on 'paropkari atma'. We should all strive to become such a soul. The gist of her talk was:

- Do not see bad in others
- If you do see the bad, do not let it disturb your mind
- Those who speak against you or manipulate against you deserve your compassion and not your hatred, for you can imagine how insecure that person is
- Do not listen to bad talk about yourself or others – if you have to as the mediator call the other person and hear his point of view too
- Give but without expectations of any returns

She gave the example of people who say *'Main hi kyun adjust karti rahoon. Voh ek baar jhuk jaye toh main das baar jhukne ko taiyyar hun* (Why should I be adjusting all the time. If he bends once I am willing to bend ten times). You must understand that that person is bankrupt in that particular emotion and has nothing to give. You don't tell a beggar '*Tuhi mujhe ek rupiya dega toh main tujhe paanch rupiye doonga* (You give me one rupee; I'll give you five rupees).'

I had adjusted to this form of bankruptcy before MS's disease and was leading a relatively peaceful life. During those times my problems were mine – backache, migraine, the stress of difficult surgeries and hospital politics; his indifference had taught me to fend for myself. After he passed on, someone told me it was good that I had become self-sufficient during my marriage and would have no trouble now. Indeed! It is like putting a child to work so that he becomes an efficient adult worker. What about his lost childhood? Did I have to miss out on forty years of marital bliss to become proficient in managing alone after he was no more? I could have done with hugs and cuddles, love and laughter during my long marriage so that I had a tidy stock of happy memories to fall back on. The paucity of such memories meant that I would be exchanging but one form of loneliness for another. As for managing by myself, I would have perforce learnt to do so when I was eventually alone.

7.9.15

I had seen MS rubbing his side with anti-inflammatory ointment daily, fretting over his ever-changing bowel habits, but could not bear to see him groan with abdominal pain early in the morning as he was doing today. I put my arms around him.

'God, please don't make him suffer,' I prayed with all my heart.

8.9.15

Imagine raising your head from your pillow one morning and leaving your hair behind! MS's hair began to fall in bunches from head and beard, a side effect of chemo that he had been spared during the first round. Masses of grey hair lay on the pillow. It was a terrifying sight. For the first time in my life, I saw my husband's chin and jawline! Chemo had stripped a hirsute Sikh of his lush beard. He was devastated, as if denuded of his identity. The eight hours surgery, the stormy post-operative days in the ICU, even the prognosis did not shake him as much as this. The loose motions, low-grade fever, weight loss, weakness that came with this round of chemotherapy, he bore bravely, but turning into a bald, beardless Sikh was traumatising. He felt naked, vulnerable. He had managed to hide his disease from his patients till now but this was like a placard proclaiming it to the public in bold letters. No medical college teaches a doctor how to deal with a situation like this – trivial in itself but with a profound psychological impact. And when the patient is a doctor and his wife a doctor, it does not make it any easier.

'We'll do something about it,' I said.

I remembered jotting down a number from a pamphlet stuck to the wall of ACH stating 'We make wigs'. I rang them up and learnt that they had nothing to replace facial hair.

'Try a drama company,' came a helpful suggestion. I slammed down the phone.

There is something called a 'thata' that Sikh men wear to keep their beard in place after fixing it with the gooey Fixo. It is a long piece of white cloth worn over the chin and cheeks and tied on the head, till the 'fixed' beard is dried with a hair dryer. After this the thata is carefully removed and the beard remains pressed in place. To hasten the drying process, a black net was being used nowadays as a thata. I told MS to use this as a fake beard. To our surprise it worked; as for his bald pate, his turban covered it and he was happy.

12.9.15

I have started making spontaneous gestures of affection towards him as I feel compassion, sorrow and a pitying love for MS, who is now helpless and totally under my care. It took cancer to make me feel so. He continues to revert to his obnoxious ways the moment he gets a little better, but these days I forgive easily and forget fast.

13.9.15

Ruby was celebrating her grandson Aman's birthday. Though it was a Sunday, MS wanted us to go late as he was tired. This was a man who was never too tired to go to his clinic every evening on the weekdays. Instead of flaring up as I am wont to do, I told him gently, 'I have given up so many things for you, so do not make me abstain from the simple pleasure of attending a birthday party when you can easily lie down in their house.'

He agreed and for a while I forgot the travails of our life. Aman was watching a magic show with his little friends with wide-eyed wonder. Time enough for the little ones to be disillusioned later. I enjoyed their enjoyment and their food (pizza, burger) though there was healthy, tasty stuff for adults. MS ate sparingly and lay down in their bedroom to rest. I had worn a Western dress, which I rarely do. It felt nice to be appreciated.

14.9.15

Before leaving for his next chemo, I asked MS to hand me his watch, ring and kara for safekeeping at home as he had to remove them anyway at the hospital. He looked at me as if I were a dacoit robbing him at gunpoint!

There was a huge water bill he had to pay and he insisted on being driven to the office himself as he did not want to hand over such a large sum to me or the driver. He had been swindled by a person who, for a fee, would pay people's bills online as most were ignorant of this mode of monetary transactions. It saved them the time and energy of going to the respective offices. It was only after MS got a hefty bill, which included arrears of previous unpaid bills, that he realised that he had been duped as had a lot of others. As for the man, a patient, he disappeared without a trace.

Ever on the lookout for a few extra minutes of sleep, I decided to join them later by metro and get down near the office from where we could go to the hospital together. He had given me wrong instructions so I got down at the wrong metro station. After an angry exchange on the phone, I finally spotted him, a frail, old Sikh with a large turban, a shrunken face half hidden in a mask (no one wore them in the pre-COVID days), waiting for me at the bottom of the metro station stairs. On seeing me, he began spewing venom. My perspective had changed and I had begun to rejoice in his horrible manner as it meant that he was 'normal', but today I was incensed beyond measure. He was the one at fault and scolded me for being late. Our bickering continued in the car oblivious to the driver, till a big, fat striped aedes mosquito distracted me and I could rest only after I had killed it. We could do without dengue at this stage of our lives.

It was almost noon when we reached the hospital for chemo. We met the CEO of the hospital in the corridor. He recognised me immediately, for he had been the CEO of my hospital earlier. He was kind enough to escort us to the day-care ward and introduce me to the doctors, who knew me already, though now they paid special attention to us. Delay in admission was immediately rectified, for he rang up the front office to tell them that we were known to the CEO. I was overwhelmed by the new status and new power I had suddenly acquired.

MS lay down on the only remaining bed near the aisle, which I usually avoided on the days we came early. It offered no privacy if MS wet his bed. Moreover, the nurse kept asking me to move my chair whenever she attended to the patient on the adjoining bed. MS was first given drugs to prevent reaction and side effects, which was followed by chemo – carboplatin was the flavour of the day. This went on till 4 p.m. I was tired of sitting, my back ached and jokingly I told MS that he had rested enough and now it was my turn to lie down.

'*Main uth jaana* (I'll get up),' he said and we both burst out laughing.

This time, I did not feel like writing on the computer and my dairy was up to date, activities I usually pursued in between tending to MS during chemo sessions. So while MS slept, I began talking to people around me. There was a story in each one of them that needed to be tapped; they too felt better after unburdening their stories.

My heart went out to the little boy with thickly oiled hair and Malvika-lined eyes, who was yelling with pain and fright as the nurse began his chemo. His mother held him stoically, her eyes long since dried of tears. The Malvika smudged around his eyes making him look like a raccoon. He had blood cancer.

A patient's husband, who was lovingly taking care of her, asked me, 'How do you cope with your husband's illness?'

'*Ji bhar ke seva karo aur baqi bhagwan pe chod do* (I look after him to the best of my ability and leave the rest to God),' I replied.

A pleasant lady in pink had come for her father-in-law's chemo and told me that he had metastatic cancer of liver and bone; the doctors had given him less than two months to live. As he was a hypochondriac, who rang up his eighty-year-old sister in Punjab after every sneeze or cough, they had decided not to let him know that he had cancer, lest he died of dread.

'*Bande de muh de age sher bithaan da ki phayada – ke hune katiya, hune katiya. Billi kyun na bithai* (No point making a tiger sit in front of a person and keep him in perpetual fear of being bitten. Why not put a cat there instead?).' Wise thinking indeed!

The doctor had been kind enough to play along and told the old man that they were replacing the decreased liquid in his bones with these drugs.

As we waited in the lounge for the driver to bring the car, we saw mutilated wrecks of human beings flit by. Those without hair abounded, as if it was the latest fashion statement. Suddenly there was a flurry of activity at the gate. The staff was galvanised into action and from a vehicle was unloaded an emaciated, comatose old man on a stretcher. He was rushed to the ICU, where they tried to pump life into his body. I wondered if he was finally relieved of his sufferings or lingered on in no-man's land. I vowed that if ever I found MS in such a state, I would let him go in peace.

15.9.15

Today was a repeat of the chemo drug Paclitaxel that had spray-painted our house with MS's shit last time. Determined to avoid a repeat performance, I asked the doctor to take strong measures.

'*Main dhakan laga doonga* (I will put a stopper),' he laughed.

So strong were the reinforcements against a shower of shit that we now confronted the other end of the spectrum – constipation. Without compunction from 3.30 a.m. onward MS disturbed my sleep intermittently with his 'shit saga'.

'No motion.'

'Feel like passing stools but unable to do so.'

'Walked up and down for fifteen minutes but no result.'

I was invited to take part in the Kasauli literature festival. It was the highlight of my literary career. Boarding, lodging and transportation for me and a companion would be paid for. I might never get such an opportunity again but MS's chemo fell on those days. Tentatively, I asked his doctor if it could be postponed for a couple of days; he agreed. I was jubilant.

4.10.15

Simar arrived today for a six-month deputation for his hotel's Gurgaon property and could be permanently transferred here later. I hoped he would help with his father's cancer treatment. As luck would have it, MS's chemo fell on the day Simar was to report for work. Also, he would set up house in Gurgaon, instead of living with us and commuting up and down, as a lot of people did.

5.10.15

Slept fitfully; got up every so often to pee, which alternated with MS's peeing. Woke up at 7 a.m. unrefreshed and tired. Saw Simar off to work after ardaas, during which I had to pick up Choco as he howled and whined whenever we assembled in prayer with packed bags by the door as he did not want anyone to leave.

Wearily I went with MS to restart his chemo routine at the hospital. Thankfully, I had persuaded him to stop wearing suits, shoes and a turban, which took that much more time and effort to change; instead, he wore kurta pyjama, slippers and a patka. A bad case of halitosis to begin with, he forgot to brush his teeth today. Neither did he use the mouthwash prescribed to prevent oral infection that could spread through his weakened body. As if the upper end of his alimentary canal was not enough to assault on my olfactory senses, another missile was directed towards my nose by the results of an enema he received before chemo. MS had not passed stools for two days and the doctor had asked him not to strain. I could barely sit next to him but waited on him hand and foot, performing chores like:

- Raising the head end of the bed and helping him put his specs on before meals
- Lowering the head end of the bed and removing his specs after he had finished
- Stopping the drip and accompanying him to the toilet every so often as the IV fluids, diabetes and poor bladder control made him want to pee every hour
- Standing outside the men's toilet till he finished
- Attaching the drip again after he returned
- Calling the nurse when the blocked cannula needed flushing
- Giving him water to wet his dry mouth

By the time we finished, I was too exhausted even to sit up in the car, so I lay down on the back seat. After resting for a mere thirty minutes, I left for my evening OPD.

Sauruv had gone to his village for a few days as his mother was ill. His wife, Kamla, took over his duties and performed them with ill grace. The 'sourpuss in a hurry' would be impatient to go back and tend to her children while MS would take all the time in the world to come to the dining table as he did not like to eat in bed. He ate slowly and wanted the next roti fresh off the tawa only after he finished his first, which took ages. Kamla would stand at the kitchen door sullenly watching him nibble his food.

6.10.15

I got up at 7.30 a.m. after a refreshing sleep. Kamla served us an unappetising breakfast and packed my lunch for we were to go for the next cycle of chemo. My heart broke on seeing the three-year-old with leukaemia again. Had I known he was coming, I would have got chocolates for him. He was playful as a pup till the drip started and then he cried for at least one hour. I tried to regale him with cartoons on my cell and the nurse got him a pen and paper to draw; he kicked us all away. I moved around the ward playing the good Samaritan, stopping the drip of at least two people when their bottle was empty and their relatives were away (to the washroom or for paperwork) and called the nurse to change their bottles.

The uppermost button of MS's hospital shirt was undone and it fell off his bony shoulder. When he wanted to use the toilet, I told him to button up.

'*Apna sexy look auron ko mat dikhao* (Don't show your sexy look to others), lest they get attracted to my handsome husband,' I joked.

'After all, I am Mr India,' he said, adding, 'in the reverse,' as he flexed his wasted biceps wrapped in sagging, wrinkled skin. I laughed at the incongruity.

7.10.15

MS was fast losing his strength. Wasted, weak and weepy after the last chemo, he was all skull, with a wizened face, teeth stained yellow with betadine mouthwash shimmering through a sparse moustache. His neck could not bear the weight of his head that drooped like a withering flower. In the evening he drank glutamine, whey protein and Naturlax for various cancer-related issues. As I was mixing the last concoction for him, I said, '*Aaj kal aap peete bahut ho* (These days you drink a lot).'

And he replied, '*Peete hain to jeete hai* (Because I drink, I am).' And we both laughed.

At night, I sat by his side and put my arm across his far shoulder, my head on the adjacent one and sighed deeply.

Though I tried to control my emotions, tears began to slide down my cheeks. MS put his hand to my face and uttered the famous Rajesh Khanna's dialogue in the movie *Amar Prem*, 'Pushpa, I hate tears.'

8.10.15

His health had plummeted to dismal depths. But he valiantly continued trying to manage.

'If this is my condition after three chemos, how will I tolerate the other three?' he said.

Well, he had the choice to discontinue the treatment. After all, it offered only palliation, not cure. The only purpose it served was to prolong his suffering but the decision had to come from him, lest he think that I was fed up with looking after him.

Amrit was not sitting idle either. From Bengaluru, she was getting some distant pranic healing done at four hundred rupees per sitting, which, according to her, would be effective only if MS paid the money. As expected, the last bit did not go down well with her brother. She rang him up thrice a day, disturbing his sleep, as she desperately wanted him to believe in its healing powers, but only after chemo failed could we, in desperation, seek alternative therapy.

9.10.15

Now that the swimming season was over, I joined yoga classes for my physical, mental and spiritual health. It felt good to be in a totally different milieu, away from the gloomy atmosphere at home. Here, a bunch of housewives exchanged recipes, in-law woes, children's issues and husbands' idiosyncrasies in between asanas. We did pranayama, which involved various types of deep breathing exercises that filled our lungs and thereby our organs with oxygen so that every cell felt tinglingly alive. There were relaxation techniques, a sort of suggestive hypnosis which made tensions and worries seep out, replacing them with a seamless ocean of bliss and peace. Here, we ate healthy Ayurveda foods like a salad of boiled methi seed sprouts and amla with chopped tomatoes and a bit of salt. Of the two boiled amlas I was entitled to each day, I brought one home for MS.

Amrit rang up to ask if he was eating properly. He replied he did because the daroga (police) forced him to do so. He meant me of course.

'*Daroga ki kadar karte ho* (Do you value the services of the police)?' she asked, to which he replied, 'Yes.'

'When, how?' I questioned him, my face near the phone for her to hear.

At this, he told her, '*Aapas me hamare phut na dalwao* (Don't create a rift between us).'

Sauruv had returned and with him his wife's good humour. Though he was resting because of the fatigue of a fifteen-hour bus journey and sore bum after sitting on hard seats, she sang while she made crisp besan pooda today (after the horrible food she had fed us all these days) that MS ate with relish. She even tolerated MS's dilly-dallying good-humouredly, saying, '*Papaji, aajkal aap sote hee rehte ho* (Papaji, you sleep all the time these days).'

To this he replied, '*Main Kumbhkaran ban gaya hoon* (I have become Kumbhkaran),' and they returned to the easy banter they used to exchange earlier.

In between patients in my evening OPD, I went to the chamber of a bubbly colleague, Roma, for a change of mood. I had worn a mangalsutra to thumb my nose at fate for wanting to snatch this particular piece of jewellery from me. She stared at my neck without saying a word; perhaps, in deference to my precarious 'married status'.

'I have come specifically to show you this,' I blurted out.

'That's the way to go, gal,' she said, with a thumbs-up sign.

We talked shop – lazy juniors, idiosyncratic patients, one went into a sulk because I could not remember (I had enough on my mind) why I had sent her to the neurologist; she thought that I did not care enough. Another left, because my hospital was charging one and a half times the normal rates for a 'muhurat baby' – a baby that has to be delivered on a particular date and time, fixed by a pandit, there being no compelling obstetric reason to do so! Such 'muhurat babies' were the bane of our lives, for we were being forced to perform caesareans at odd hours just because it was auspicious. This particular woman wasn't some illiterate housewife but a vigilance officer.

Roma told me about the emergency surgery she had to perform on a patient with a twisted ovarian tumour before the insurance papers could be processed though she had sent an email to the concerned authorities. There was a denial from the insurance company and the patient refused to pay up, and the doctor was held responsible!

'This is what we get for saving patients' lives,' she fumed. I felt like hugging her when she added, 'My mother must be looking after me from heaven, for I do not know what prompted me to send the mail that eventually saved me.' Her mother was a patient of depression, who eventually committed suicide.

'I agree, we don't usually send such mails.'

We had been talking for some time when MS rang up to say, '*Aa gayi,*' and I replied, '*Mubarak ho, Piku.*'

'Piku?' asked Roma, curious.

I told her that his shit was a subject of constant concern in our household, like Amitabh Bachchan's in the movie *Piku*. 'My husband has become so dependent that like a child he now wants a pat on the back for his excretory feat.'

11.10.15

MS grew weaker day by day. He took to groaning constantly when in bed. I would lie down without covering myself, hot after my daily activities. After a while when my BMR (basal metabolic rate) settled and I began to feel cold, MS would cover me with a sheet/blanket/quilt according to the season. That was something I would really miss.

Though he had stopped going to his morning OPD a long time back, I told him to stop his evening OPD too but he said that he could not ditch his patients. They would find another doctor soon enough once he was out of circulation but I did not tell him that. Instead, I started sending Sunita, one of my nurses, along to keep an eye on him. As she was more efficient than his new compounder, she saved MS the effort of filling and giving injections, taking BP, temperature, etc. She would tell me that the OPD was usually full, as he charged so little. It gladdened my heart to learn that his patients loved him and he had such a way with children that they would not even notice when he gave them an injection. But how come he never showed that aspect of his personality to me?

12.10.15

This time chemo squeezed him dry. His haemoglobin level was reduced to 9 g/dL and he developed low-grade temperature, yet MS would rest to conserve energy during the day so that he could go to the clinic in the evening. Actually, when he wore pants and a full-sleeved shirt that covered his wasted limbs, he did not look as wasted as he really was.

13.10.15

The future of the corporate hospital I was working in was uncertain and so was mine, for the professional fate of all the doctors working there was linked with its fate. As these premises were rented and as another sprawling superspeciality branch had come up on purchased land, they were whittling down the services offered here. Of the ten floors they rented, they retained only three, on one of which only a day-care centre would function. This meant that we had to take our admissions to the other branch, which was some distance away. Even as this weighed upon my mind, I performed a caesarean late at night and returned at 2 a.m. I caught up with whatever sleep I could and missed yoga so that MS would not have to miss his appointment with the oncologist. As he tired easily it took much effort and time to get him dressed. Somehow I managed to ready both MS and his papers when I got a call for another emergency, which my stand-in was unable to manage. Though the patient gave me a few palpitations with the foetal heart rate going haywire, we managed to deliver her big-sized baby vaginally. We rescheduled the consult for the next day. I really wished Simar was here to take care of his father and told him so when he rang up next. Of what use was a posting in the NCR if he was not there when we needed him?

14.10.15

Simar took an off today, for which I was glad as another emergency cropped up. I handed him a weakened father, his hospital records and a paper on which I had written what he should ask the doctor about MS's:

- Fever
- Weight loss
- Constipation
- Severe weakness
- Decreased haemoglobin
- Need for blood

I also asked him to fill the insurance form for three days' admission with PET scan and chemo, instead of daycare.

MS had refused PET on an OPD basis, which would have been more cost-effective. Also, if it revealed that MS was beyond treatment, the insurance companies would not pay hospitalisation charges for mere investigations. In his debilitated state, the doctor said that a PET scan could only be done if his blood sugar was less than 160, liver and kidney function tests normal. Simar also donated blood for his father in case it was necessary to transfuse him.

That night after a long time I went to see a movie at a fancy theatre with Simar and brought pizza and garlic bread home to share with MS.

15–17.10.15

MS tires easily – after a bath, a meal, after using the washroom. The constipation was corrected by increasing the dose of his herbal stool softener to twice a day. Thankfully, that was one litany out of the way. Reading *Being Mortal* by Atul Gawande raised a lot of questions.

Doctors are either 'doctor knows best' or give an array of information leaving to the patient the difficult task of choosing. They are taught to cure diseases, fix surgical problems, prolong life even if it means prolonging the agony and decreasing the quality of life. Patients with terminal cancer remain either in a state of perpetual grogginess or on ventilators with tubes in every orifice natural/unnatural. No one teaches them to ask how the patient wants to die or other hard questions like:

- What sort of life do you want in the remaining time in the given circumstances?
- Where do you want to die – at home among those who love you or in the hospital, where impersonal, efficient robot-like people probe and prod you?
- Do you want to be resuscitated when the time arises?
- What are you willing to trade off for what you want?

- Do you want third-line chemo with more side effects and dubious results?

This made me think, for we were approaching that crossroad soon – in fact, on the 26th, when the PET scan would show us whether three cycles of second-generation chemo had done their job after extracting so heavy a price.

Frail and shrunken, in a vest and shorts, MS lay in the favourite position on the side with his head at the foot end of the bed. His shrunken cheek and bald skull resting on his folded arm, his thin thighs and his knobby knees folded in the foetal position. I was to remember him in this pitiable state for days to come.

I too sat as usual at the head end of the bed facing him. My back rested on pillows placed against the bedstead while my laptop rested on a low table on the bed in front. He looked at me bleakly but did not utter a word. At times, my feet touched his hand inadvertently and he would pull it away. After much hesitation, I gathered courage to ask him the one question that was bothering me. I had to know what he wanted in case the PET report was not good. This, Karan had said, was a given with the painfully enlarged liver, though I did not tell MS that. I began by emphasising that what he wanted was the most important thing for us and we would be with him one hundred per cent. I gave him a summary of the book and said that there was a man mentioned in it who could become quadriplegic after surgery. When his daughter asked him if this was acceptable, he replied, 'As long as I am able to watch football on TV and eat chocolate ice cream, I would like to live.' So the choice is completely yours, I told him, as regards the continuation of palliative chemo.

He looked at me like a lamb at a butcher but did not utter a word. After a prolonged pause, I began in a different vein.

'It's high time you stop acting like a baby. You have just given up, not caring to read up or ask about the course of the disease, its prognosis, the quality of life with or without chemo, though you are both doctor and patient at the same time. This is not the time for procrastinating. You have got to tell us what you want from the limited time you have at your disposal so that we can decide accordingly.'

He did not answer. To give him another perspective, I added, 'For all you know, I could die before you, but your symptoms are more apparent, you have to make some hard choices as has been mentioned in this book that Karan specifically asked me to read.'

A silent tear trickled down his eye to pool in the hollow made by his specs on the side of his nose. My heart went out to him and I berated myself for cornering him so hard-heartedly. It was difficult coming to terms with one's mortality without my rubbing it in.

I did not tell him that 50 to 60 per cent of caregivers go into depression afterwards, for he couldn't care less. In fact, I was already halfway there, but as long as I could look after him, it did not matter.

The electricity bill arrived that very afternoon and cancer or no cancer all hell broke loose. MS did have the knack of converting compassion into loathing in two minutes flat. He started yelling at me, and I at the help (the cooler in his room was on 24/7), who threatened to leave. If only I had the option of leaving.

'This is what you get by saying anything to them. I am the only one on whom you can vent your anger because you know I will not leave you in this state,' I fumed.

At this he changed tactics and began whining. 'I hardly earn anything these days. You must share the bill with me.'

Did he not see that his cancer had drained my resources? Moreover, that neglecting my practice to chaperone him to the hospital repeatedly had decreased my income?

20.10.15

Karan thought it was commendable that Simar had decided to shift base to be with his father. I dared not ruffle their feathers by saying it was too little, too late. He also deposited one and a half lakh rupees in my account for 'Papa's treatment', adding that we should keep a driver for Simar or give him half the money. He was already telling me how to spend the paltry sum he had sent. I hoped and prayed that I would never have to depend on my sons for anything till my dying day. Keeping my thoughts to myself, I said, 'It would be better if we kept it for later; if and when MS becomes bedridden and we have to keep male attendants for him round the clock.'

'It's but a matter of months with liver metastasis,' he said.

My heart gave a jolt. No matter how much you feel you are prepared for such an eventuality, you never really are. When I shared Karan's prognosis with Simar, I could see that he was shaken. Little did we know then that MS had less than a month to live.

MS sat on the terrace in the morning, earnestly doing the yogic 'Oooooom' to take in as much oxygen as possible. With the prominent groove on the base of his nose where he perched his specs, his myopic eyes bulging, the pallor of his skin striking, his large, naked skull and pinched face, he looked as grotesque as a gnome. This pathetic attempt at survival smote my heart, for he was beyond help now.

How awful it must be for a person to know that he is dying. How awful to contemplate that his loved ones were thinking of stopping chemo, in case the PET scan showed it was not working; to be talked about in third person as he refused to take any decisions himself. How awful for him to write his will; it was akin to signing a death warrant for a person of his temperament. I had ultimately persuaded him to do so on an A4 sheet with the two nurses as witnesses. Though it was neither on stamp paper nor registered, it was better than not having any, in case a legal issue arose.

His world revolves around his motions and low-grade evening fever. The whole day he lies in bed too weak to even pick up the phone. Having a bath is tiring, as is getting up for meals, yet to his credit he rouses himself every evening with a strong cup of coffee and a tablet of Modafinil to go to the clinic; no one else could have done it. He returns bone-tired and throws himself on the bed sleeping for at least thirty minutes before he can gather the strength to have his dinner.

22.10.15

Karva Chauth was approaching, Sauruv got a sari worth two thousand rupees for Kamla, Jagdish got one costing three thousand for Sunita, Simar got Mona a gold set for 1.6 lakh, but MS bought nothing for me, though he knew this would be our last Karva Chauth. I was foolish to revive expectations from a stone-hearted man (who would soon be leaving behind the money he had hoarded), but seeing a driver's and a domestic help's wife fare better than me was more than I could bear. I had so much wanted something nice to remember him by. I almost told him what I thought of him but refrained. Paltry sounded my demand for a gift in the present circumstances. He could continue being his obnoxious self as long as he did not suffer. That was all I wanted from him, for him.

Yet, I cannot help wonder that if I had happy memories to sustain me, I would not be thus demeaning a dead man who could not defend himself. All I can say in my defence is that I had to get it all out of my system like a woman in labour or die in the process.

25.10.15

The penultimate day of the PET scan verdict was Sunday the 26th. I decided to make the most of it and took MS to see a slapstick comedy that he so enjoyed. Dinner was at Radisson Blue as I was a panellist at the 'Clinic to Court' conference held there. Though distracting, the coming morrow lay in the dark recesses of my mind like a coiled snake waiting to strike. Simar had taken leave to accompany us to the hospital and was sleeping at home when we returned.

26.10.15

MS groaned the whole night. When I asked him if he was in pain, he said, '*Nahin, ghabrahat ho rahi hai* (No, I am uneasy).' The words of consolation I muttered seemed so inadequate. We were all up by 6 a.m. As MS was a diabetic, he was allowed an early light breakfast before PET. Simar insisted that I come later, after getting the house cleaned before locking it up. I could sense that MS wanted me by his side.

'Simar may not be able to manage,' he began.

I reminded him that a PET scan takes a couple of hours and all that Simar or for that matter I would do in the meantime was wait outside with his belongings. We had been through it earlier and he knew.

'I'll be there by the time it is over,' I assured him.

He kept quiet, so I asked, 'If you want me to come along for moral support, say so, I'll come.'

He did not answer. How could he? During all our time together, he was never there for me during any medical emergency. This was not the time to take petty revenge, but even if I went along, I would not be able to hold his hand as he would be inside. Meanwhile, now that we had Simar, I could get much done at home.

I reached the hospital as soon as I could. The scan over, MS had been shifted to his room. I decided to meet the oncologist before going to him. At my request the good doctor rang up the radiologist for some verbal information as it would take time to get the written report. We learnt that though the lymph nodes and the adrenal gland lesions had regressed, the liver metastasis had increased.

'How is this possible?'

'It depends upon the sensitivity of individual organs.' Later, Karan told me that certain cancer cells mutate and become resistant to chemo.

Simar and I were having our packed lunch of gobhi parathas with pickle, seated on the settee by MS's side. Suddenly, the settee, the bed, the TV and the fridge in the room began to shake. This went on for what seemed a full five minutes and on the TV the news flashed.

There had been an earthquake – 7.7 on the Richter scale with an epicentre in the Hindu Kush mountains in Afghanistan. Here I was feeling sorry for MS when I did not know what would happen to all of us in the next few seconds. It did not occur to either of us to desert MS and run for our lives.

After an hour or so, we went to meet the oncologist again. He avoided eye contact, shuffling papers, till I was forced to ask him if he had seen the films. He told me that he had and the liver mets had grown to double their size! I was shocked at the rapid progress in six weeks. With a clinically palpable liver we had been expecting this all along, yet hoping against hope. It was as if I had been expecting to fail all along but to see it in black and white on the report card came as a shock.

'What now?' I asked.

'We can go back to gemcitabine and carboplatin.'

'What purpose will that serve? If the second line of chemo has not worked, how will this help.'

'We can try,' he said, not very convincingly.

'What if we opt out?'

'That is also an option. Why don't you send the report to your son, the liver specialist abroad, and let me know what you decide?' I took pictures of the report and sent them to Karan.

When the doctor came for the evening round, I asked him, 'What will happen if we opt out?'

'He can have jaundice, ascites which will need tapping ...'

'But in the daycare, I have seen so many patients with needles in their abdomens and thorax tapping fluid, despite the chemo.'

'Yes,' he agreed.

'Will he have pain?'

'Yes, it could be due to stretching of the liver capsule or if he gets bone metastasis.'

'What will we do then?'

'Give local radiation.'

Simar hugged me, uttering a dialogue from the movie *Devdas*, '*Chunnilal, hum la-elaaj ho gaye* (Chunnilal, I am beyond treatment now),' which said it all.

Karan rang up in the afternoon to say what I knew he would.

'There is no point in torturing him further with chemo. It is not going to help and the side effects are bad.'

'Yes.'

'Where are you now?'

'I have just come home. Simar will be staying with Papa for the night.'

'I suggest you go back, so that we can break the news to him together.'

'OK.'

27.10.15

MS was discharged today after much red-tapism. The discharge slip mentioned that we refused chemo, which could go against us with the insurance company and though the oncologist changed it to, 'As the disease progressed, palliation advised at home', we were refused claim. This was because the company paid for treatment and not investigations and all we had got done after admission was a PET scan. So Simar paid thirty thousand rupees from his pocket for the hospital stay, when an outpatient PET scan would have been way cheaper, but that was not the issue right now. What troubled us now was how to manage MS at this delicate juncture.

As before, MS remained in a state of denial. He uttered not a word about the prognosis or our decision but began his 'motion' saga once again. Even after an enema at the hospital, a sense of incomplete evacuation prevailed. This made him very uncomfortable till the Ayurvedic medicine worked its magic and much to his satisfaction he evacuated his bowels completely.

28.10.15

My role was now passive – to make MS as comfortable as possible while nature took its course. He was too weak to do anything but sleep most of the time. Slowly, steadily I began preparing myself for a future without him.

2.11.15

After a long time, I went for a gynaecological workshop with a colleague.

'Your smile does not reach your eyes these days,' she said.

I smiled wanly and said nothing.

She was tall and dark while her husband was short and fair. Though they made an incongruous pair, she loved him dearly, even after years of marriage.

‘What is it that you love most about him?’ I asked. ‘Romance, gifts, sex, companionship?’

‘I am not interested in those things. What turns me on is intellect, of which he has plenty.’

‘And a very handsome income,’ I added inwardly. In short, he was a husband she looked up to and I was glad for her.

While on our way back, the nurse rang up to say that MS was drenched in sweat, his eyes had rolled upwards and he was not responding. I began crying in the cab while she added, ‘BP, pulse is normal,’ which was impossible.

Keeping my pain on hold, I asked her to check his blood sugar levels. They were very low. I told her to start a 5 per cent dextrose drip while I got 25 per cent and 10 per cent glucose en route from my hospital – a member of the staff would be waiting with them on the road. I rang up the children too and Simar had already started from Gurgaon. After a while MS began responding, so Simar turned back from Dhaula Kuan as his hotel was very busy during the Diwali season. It had been an utterly exhausting day that left me completely drained.

3.11.15

MS’s blood sugars fell again in the morning. I gave him a shot of 25 per cent glucose and started a 10 per cent glucose drip. Erratic blood sugar level was but one of his problems; his electrolytes were low and I gave appropriate injections after a tele-consult with his doctor. No shit for two days, which was his one major concern. Perhaps the cancer had invaded his brain, for there was intermittent loss of memory and slurred speech. Karan told me that this was ‘chemo brain’, a horrifying side effect of these horrible drugs. I found him seated on a stool in the bathroom, a pathetic figure desperate for a bath but unable to muster the strength to do so – he who bathed twice a day! While helping him bathe, I shook his soapy right hand with mine and said, 'Glad to meet you, sir,' at which he gave a wan smile.

MS wet his bed completely as he had become too weak to change diapers. Instead, he put a thick wad of newspaper over the wet area and slept again. Though I felt sorry for him, I was too tired to move, my back hurt on bending and the two of us just lay there unable to do a thing. As for Simar, though he shifted to be with us, he was based in Gurgaon and did not actually help with the day-to-daycare of the invalid. Even if he'd lived with us, he suffered from disc prolapse and could not nurse his father physically. The time had come to hire extra help.

Even in this state, the clinic was his priority. He was in no condition to go and I told him so categorically; he would only harm himself and his patients and that was totally unjustifiable. The moment my back was turned, he gave the help the key of his almirah (something he never gave me) to take out his pants, its pockets full of money, and dress him up. Once ready, he called for the driver Jagdish. As instructed, Sauruv said that Jagdish had gone home, but at MS's insistence he was 'called' back. On seeing him, MS said, '*Pay main deta hoon ya voh* (I give you the pay or she)?'

Ignoring the taunt, I pretended that the car key was misplaced, but such was his desire to go to the clinic that he took out the duplicate key and set off. Reluctantly, I sent the nurse along. She returned with some alarming news. MS was totally disoriented.

- He returned a hundred rupees to a patient who gave him sixty rupees
- Wrote a prescription for gas to a patient who was suffering from fever
- Examined the son but demanded charges for seeing both father and son

- While returning, he told the driver that he had taken a wrong turn when he entered our lane
- Stumbled while climbing the stairs

I did not admonish him. Exhausted, he fell on the bed, a pale mask with dry yellow teeth. Finally, late at night, he mustered the strength to get up and eat, slowly and with difficulty. I left him to perform some before-bedtime chores. On returning I saw that he had vomited into his plate. I cleaned him, consoled him and took him back to bed.

4.11.15
Once again MS bathed, dressed and insisted on going to the clinic. At my wits' end, I discussed it with Karan on the phone. He suggested that I sedate him and hide his almirah keys. I did the latter so he would not give it to the help who could take out all the cash in front of his eyes without MS being able to do a thing. Thankfully, I did not have to sedate him, for the exertion of getting ready had taken its toll and he decided to rest for fifteen minutes before leaving. Instead, he slept on and on. I let him sleep but that meant no food and his blood sugar dropped to dangerously low levels. After replenishing, I went to the hospital to get a male attendant for MS. I met Dr Roma, my confidante, and said miserably, 'I am utterly exhausted mentally, physically and emotionally; I don't know whether I am coming or going ...'

'You are not getting any younger yourself; you don't have to kill yourself.'

5.11.15
MS had thrown off the blanket but could not muster the strength to get up and go to the toilet. As a result, he was drenched in urine from calf to waist. Despite my aching back I changed his clothes, bed sheets and diapers and collapsed,

as exhausted as him. I caressed him as he lay on a clean, dry bed, but the night was not over yet. He began having pain in his abdomen so I gave him carom seeds with water as requested. Then he wanted a glass of nimbu pani, and towards morning it was sugar milk and a pinni. Finally, he slept, while I stayed awake miserable with fatigue, backache and migraine.

Simar got an unexpected off and came home. He bathed his urine-drenched father, making wisecracks that brought a grimace of a smile on MS's wan face. All spruced up, we took pictures of him alone and with us.

6.11.15

I got up with a start at 4 a.m. and was horrified to see MS curled up in the foetal position on the floor. I thought he had fallen down, but learnt that he had gone to the toilet with the aid of a torch (he could not sleep with the night light on) and inadvertently left it there. As he could not find the way back to his bed in the dark, he lay down on the floor. This shook me up more than anything else. I woke up Simar, who helped me put his disoriented dad back on the bed. I woke up a while later to check on MS and found him huddled in bed with his torch on and blanket on the floor for another trip to the toilet which he was unable to make and he had wet his bed again. As for Simar, he left for work. All his sympathy and care had dissipated in a day, during which he was impatient, patronising and harsh with me.

When Karan rang up, I told him of the fast-deteriorating condition of his father and said that February would be too late as he had applied for leave then.

'Should I come now?'

'I think so.'

Even as we were talking, he booked the tickets. 'Will come on Sunday and stay till Friday.'

What gave MS an inkling of his deteriorating condition was our decision to shift him downstairs to the nursing home. Bewildered, he stumbled down the stairs. I had managed to arrange two male GDAs (general duty attendants, a fancy corporate name for ayahs) to look after him for twelve hours each. Paramjit would come later to supervise them. After feeding MS, I left him at the mercy of the GDA and instructing the night nurse to watch over MS, I went upstairs.

7.11.15
I slept without disturbance for the first time in a month and felt guilty about it. In the morning I learnt that MS mumbled the whole night and did not sleep a wink. He was disoriented and did not know where he was or with whom. The GDA Sagar said that he had to change his diaper several times. Though he had been fed milk with a pinni, MS complained to me, as a child would to a mother, that it was 7 p.m. and no one had given him tea or anything to eat. I pulled the curtains apart to let him know it was morning.

Paramjit came from Nainital and was shocked when his chachu asked him, '*Tussi kaun ho, Sardarji? Kithon aye ho* (Who are you Sardarji, where have you come from?)' This made him howl and cry and he sat glued to his chachu's bedside. When I came downstairs MS said, '*Chalo chalein* (Let's go).'

He wanted me to take him upstairs to his own bed. I put my head on his shoulder and cried, for he would never sleep in his own bed again. Instead, I brought Choco down to meet MS. I sat on the sofa by his bed and prayed. After a while MS began calling out for Jessy, our precious grandson. I rang up Mona and asked her to bring him to Delhi so that his grandfather could see him one last time. She said that their tickets were booked for the 27th and they would come then. It would be too late but how could I force someone who refused to understand the urgency of the situation. Happily,

MS mistook Ruby's grandson for our grandson and played with him when they came visiting one day.

Paramjit's duty was to oversee the activities of the GDA on night duty lest he sleep and neglect MS. He came upstairs, begging me to bring MS upstairs as he desperately wanted to come back to his own room. I told him that it was impossible as I could not sleep in the same room with a strange male attendant. Even if I shifted to the other bedroom, seeing that I was the only one in the house with the invalid, he could rob and kill us without a qualm. Senior citizens were soft targets for mercenary murderers in Delhi as one often read in the newspapers. Another important reason to keep him in the nursing home was the fact that the nurses could monitor his temperature, pulse, BP, blood sugar and give him the requisite medicines.

'What do I tell him when he begs me to take him upstairs?' said a teary-eyed Paramjit.

'Very well, then, I'll bring him upstairs on the condition that you stay back with us, sleep with MS and the attendant in one room and I in another.' He had no answer to that for he could not close his shop indefinitely. He had the grace not to rub in the fact that MS had two sons of his own who could very well do the needful.

MS had barely swallowed a morsel in the afternoon; he did not eat anything at night either. As I was wondering whether to start an IV line, Karan rang up to tell me firmly to 'just let him be'. For once I was glad that Karan was all brain and no heart. In a perverse sort of way, I was even relieved that he would not let me linger on, in case I found myself in such a situation.

8.11.15

I got up at 6 a.m. and went downstairs with pinni and milk, which I was gratified to observe that MS ate though he looked worse than yesterday. Earlier, he was deteriorating every 24 hours and now, every 12 hours. I sat on the settee outside and cried and cried for I knew that the end was near. Having expended my grief for now, I asked the staff to remove the extra furniture from our 'in-house mortuary' and clean up the place. I could not afford to play the helpless, weepy widow because there was no one else to manage the shifting of the furniture.

Earlier this used to be a labour room where life was welcomed; now it served as a general ward for poor patients and intermittently was cleared to keep bodies of family members for a final darshan by relatives, before they began their last journey on a bier to the pyre. Though my mother-in-law had died a lingering death in Delhi, to our utmost horror, the lifeless forms of my father-in-law and some years later my brother-in-law made an eight-hour journey in a hearse to Delhi with relatives sitting with them in the same closed space. They preferred this to the alternative of performing the final rites in Nainital for the entire clan. Except for the mood, sombre in one and joyous in the other, the workload of a funeral was no less than that of a wedding.

Paramjit was devastated to hear MS repeatedly saying that he wanted to go home as his family was waiting for him, unaware that it was his family that had put him here. He thought it was heartless of me not to heed my husband's last wish, which made me feel guilty. At one time MS said that he saw light at the end of a tunnel and asked Paramjit if he should go. Paramjit told him to go to sleep. But I couldn't help wondering. I had read of innumerable incidences of near-death experiences when people saw a light at the end of a tunnel; MS could not have known, for he never read books.

When Simar rang up I was crying inconsolably and said that Mona might have to change her tickets to an earlier date, implying that the end was near.

'Never mind the tickets,' he cut in curtly. He didn't get it that I was trying to tell him that time was running out for his father.

'I am not in a state of mind to filter words before I speak to you,' I said and put down the phone. I did not need Simar's insensitivity to add to my woes. I had work to do and plenty of it. Karan was coming at night while Amrit was coming with her son the next day and the house was in a mess. It needed urgent cleaning to accommodate the visiting relatives.

I took MS out on a wheelchair to the driveway, made him breathe deeply of the fresh air and had a cup of tea with him (perhaps our last together) with biscuits. In the meantime I got his waterbed emptied, as it was making him uncomfortable. Moreover, it did not appear as if he would last long enough to develop bedsores. Just having tea on a wheelchair exhausted MS and we settled him back into bed. Simar arrived soon after. I decided to go with him, the driver and Sunita to MS's clinic today. As I was locking up, Ruby turned up, so I took her along too.

Sadly, I realised that this was the first time I would be visiting his clinic after he had bought and renovated it. I would say half in jest and half in sorrow that he should have got it inaugurated by his *grihalakshmi* – me, for the wife brought wealth and prosperity, as the incarnate of Goddess Lakshmi. The flooring and settees were new as were the steel almirahs. Simar looked into his drawers, Sunita for injections, while Ruby kept telling us that it was in very bad taste to plunder his shop when he was still alive.

'Just change the locks and come away,' she urged. It did appear unfeeling but the urgency to come at this inappropriate time was prompted by the fact that Sunita would be leaving with her husband – she had finally married Jagdish – to attend her sister's marriage. She knew where the vaccinations and injections were kept in the fridge, which would go to waste once the electricity was turned off. Jagdish could help Simar shift the heavier things. I also knew that when it was over, all would leave and I would have to do this alone. After removing what was essential, we turned off the mains, changed the locks and came home.

Karan reached home at 10.30 p.m. Paramjit (all heart and no brain) was a mental wreck. He would not leave MS's side the entire night (though MS did not recognise him), which made us feel guilty as if we were not doing enough for him when all he needed was loving care. He would harass the GDA, wet MS's lips intermittently and ask MS again and again if he recognised him. In short, he would not let his chachu rest in peace. On the other hand, Karan took the imminent demise of his father in his stride, saying that the two and a half years he got were a bonus.

9.11.15

MS was in pain so Karan gave him an Ultracet and another at 4 p.m. This led to a semi-comatose, unresponsive state with pinpoint pupils. He had not eaten a morsel the entire day. As it was Dhanteras and one has to buy some metal on this day, I decided to buy steel dinner sets from Big Bazaar for my employees for Diwali. I did not want to deprive them of this yearly gift if something untoward happened before the festival. They had been of immense help to us during these trying times. I wanted to reward them. I made the mistake of taking Karan along and paid dearly for it, subjected as I was to his irritation and rudeness; not that I wanted to linger, for Amrit would be arriving soon.

People would advise me to live with either of my sons once this was over as it would be difficult for an ageing woman to manage on her own. I couldn't contemplate spending the rest of my life with Karan (not that he offered) and risk being rebuffed or shouted at for every little thing. Forbearance was not one of my virtues. As for Simar, his impatience and patronising manner were beyond endurance. I was good enough to hand over my life's savings to him on a platter for the restaurant he was buying, but he would blow up if I so much as repeated something I might have said earlier. This was part of the ageing process but he had zero tolerance. As for my daughter-in-law, not only was she indifferent to our state, she was hard-hearted enough to refuse a dying man's wish to see his grandson one last time. I had no wish to live as a nursemaid and cook in her house and lose my identity as a doctor, a writer, a person in my own right. The moot point was, would I be able to manage on my own in illness and health, without a soul in the vicinity? Ruby lived just eight kilometres away and I knew that she would come to see me often. Maybe Rajan might help for old times' sake as there would be no hindrance, no guilt now.

'I'll cross that bridge when I come to it,' I thought, shaking away such contemplations.

I now dreaded the arrival of Amrit with her brand of axioms and false optimism that she passed off as positive thinking. Well, let her see for herself the effect of the long-distance pranic healing at four hundred rupees per session which MS was supposed to pay for. Being a doctor and a realist, I knew exactly where we were heading.

As his mother was emotionally labile, Amrit's elder son had come with her to give her moral support – not to look after his 'beloved' uncle, as she would like us to believe. I let it pass but told Karan about Amrit's son's concern for his mother, hoping that he would be more considerate of me. Nothing of that sort happened. The very next day when I asked him to rub the electric massager down my aching back, he told me to do it myself. As if I wouldn't have, if my hand could reach the sore spot.

Amrit hugged me and cried as MS did not recognise her and she regretted not coming earlier. Now that Amrit and Karan were there to look after MS, I decided to attend my evening clinic, dressed defiantly in a bright red sari. People may have commented behind my back but I chose to ignore them and concentrated only on the positives. Roma said that I reminded her of an article written by Twinkle Khanna called 'Red Lipstick'. It was about people she knew, chiefly her grandmother (who had seen three of her four children die) and her childhood friend who had lost her mother, all immaculately dressed and made-up, a cancer sticker included, for a hospitalised family friend who wears 'the brightest, happiest red lipstick', for she is telling the world that she is not letting her problems drag her down.

Maybe this was exactly what I was doing. As I drove back home, I was stuck in a traffic jam and out of habit came the thought, 'MS will be stuck in the traffic due to the pre-Diwali rush,' only to remember the very next instant that he was at home, ill, very ill. Life would be empty without him. It wasn't a great love that I would miss (there was no such thing between us) but the set pattern of our lives, the little things we did as a couple. It was uncanny how sometimes the radio echoes one's thoughts. I put on FM Gold on the car radio; almost immediately, in the darkness within and without echoed a song sung expressly for MS:

> *Chal ud jaa re panchi ab ye desh hua begana … teri kismet me likha hai jeete ji mar jaana …* (Go, fly away bird, this country is no longer yours … It is written in your fate to die while you still live)

A vision of MS dead while he still breathed swam before my eyes. The dam burst and scream after scream emanated from the car quite like Konkona Sen venting in the movie *Life in a Metro*. Not a soul heard … or cared. Unfamiliar, guttural sounds of grief emerged from my throat. With my heart unburdened for at least a while, I drove home and tried giving Karan an inkling of my grief. At this he quipped, 'You didn't run over someone did you?'

Unable to suppress my gift for repartee even at this juncture, I replied, 'In that case, I would have sung – *teri kismet mein likha hai meri car ke neeche mar jaana* … (it is in your fate to die under my car).'

I thought I had done enough grieving for the day, but one look at MS's wasted form and tears erupted afresh. I went upstairs to continue crying, where Karan made fun of me weeping over a partner I had resented all my life. My sister and my brother's wife would later exchange knowing looks while I shed 'crocodile tears'. As if I was playing to an audience to gain sympathy. No one understood the enormity of my loss, the gnawing void a forty-one-year-old presence could leave by its absence.

Amrit's son pretended not to know anything about the severity of MS's condition; this, when his mother received an hourly account during the thrice-a-day phone calls she made from Bengaluru. He asked questions about the disease as if he was a student of oncology and the cancer was not a monster that was rapidly devouring a family member. I looked at Amrit baffled. Did she not update her family or this was merely his idea of small talk? Either way, it was in bad taste.

Now that MS had a 'deadline' to complete 'project life', could he not audit his emotions, set his affairs in order and go with a clean slate? Could he not ask for and give forgiveness, express gratitude, open his heart, which had always remained as tightly closed as his fist? Could he not enjoy whatever was left of our togetherness? Were there no regrets, no desires left that he could not postpone? Was there no list of things he was eager to finish before he passed away? Did it not occur to him to make my transition into a life without him as easy as possible?

I mulled over the two and a half years MS had got as bonus and wondered at the way he had squandered them.

I, for one, subscribe to what some attribute to Hunter S. Thompson:

> Life should not be a journey to the grave with the intention of arriving safely in a pretty and well-preserved body, but rather to skid in broadside, thoroughly used up, totally worn out, and loudly proclaiming 'Wow! What a Ride!'

I have known cancer patients who rave and rant, and do not allow their near ones to leave their sides for a moment. As MS did not want others to know about his cancer, I had managed to ward off visitors till now, but Amrit told her cousin about MS's plight. She came running, and shocked at seeing the shrunken caricature of her once robust cousin, she left crying, only to return with a horde of other relatives. This led to a chorus of crying, while MS lay unresponsive and still with a deathly pallor on his masklike face. I am glad he did not know what was happening for it would have mortified him.

10.11.15

Amrit almost never left her brother's side during the day. She had finally given up her futile optimism and was a comfort to have around. At night, Paramjit was his usual hyper self, not sleeping a wink and not allowing the help to help. The night ward boy was thin and unable to lift MS alone, though he was more amenable to taking orders; the daytime person, though fitter and more experienced, tried to get out of smelly situations like washing MS's bottom till he was forced to do so.

The effect of tramadol had worn off and MS was more responsive. At 6.30 a.m. when I was trying to feed him some milk, Paramjit, a bundle of nerves, began shouting at me, like he would at his mother, till I gave him a piece of my mind.

'Don't you dare talk to me like this! Just go upstairs and sleep instead of making a nuisance of yourself.'

Karan felt caged and went to Connaught Place with Amrit's son; they did not stop at Bangla Sahib Gurdwara to pray for MS, as Amrit wanted them to.

Sapna had to leave for a court case in Kerala. In her place we had hired a sourpuss of a nurse, Omana, who thankfully had worked in the ICU and in an old people's home. She was more suited to the task at hand while my nurses were adept at obstetrics care.

Paramjit was leaving at night as his mother could not manage the Diwali rush at their shop. Once again, before leaving he asked me if it was possible to bring MS upstairs every morning and take him down at night. Enough was enough!

'You think you are the only one who cares? Give me one reason why I would not do what is best for him? Who has the most to lose once he is gone, you or me?'

At this he started howling. I hugged him tight and kissed him. Just then a dealer rang up and Paramjit got into a heated argument with him. As abruptly as that, he switched from our world into his own, while Karan and I looked on, amazed at the drastic transformation.

Karan derived a sadistic pleasure in hurting me during his visits, however brief. The stress of MS's illness had considerably lowered my threshold to tolerate such barbs. His words would lodge like porcupine quills in my heart. When the pain became unbearable, it would surface in the form of tears, which made him despise me all the more. It seemed that the sole purpose of his visit was to torture me.

Seeing MS's condition over the last few days, I wondered if we would be in mourning this Diwali or 'celebrating' it. Well, the festival of lights was upon our darkened world and MS was alive, though barely so. Karan told me to bathe quickly, as we had decided to go to the gurdwara in the morning before the air got polluted with fire crackers and played havoc with MS's breathing. After I finished, I knocked on his door to tell him that I had filled a bucket of hot water for him. No reply. As the water was getting cold, I knocked again after a while.

'Leave me alone,' came the curt response.

I had heard worse from him before, but my threshold for tolerance, not very high to begin with, hit rock bottom. Fed up with his insensitivity, I locked myself in my room and refused to open it when he knocked. He knocked again and said, 'Sorry.' I did not answer. He knocked again after a while, but again I did not answer. This frightened him out of his wits, for he called out to Amrit, who came rushing, fearing the worst. She was sure glad that I was not hanging from the ceiling when I opened the door at her behest. Karan tried to pass off his behaviour as stress but I knew better. First, I was way more stressed than him, and second, he had always spoken to me like that - it's just that I had retaliated differently this time.

My sister came to wish us and we exchanged gifts. Finally, Simar turned up with a Diwali gift hamper from the Oberoi and a chocolate cake – none of which I liked, but they were very expensive and very much in demand. I did not have the heart to celebrate, but as the moonless night advanced, I snapped out of my depression to initiate the festivities. After all, it would be MS's last Diwali and celebrations, not mourning, were in order.

I prepared two thalis with all the Diwali paraphernalia – Lakshmi and Ganesh, earthenware mustard oil lamps, incense sticks, rice grains, saffron, raw milk, marigold flowers, sweetmeats, a sparkler or two and coins. Being a Sikh, I added a picture of Guru Nanak for good measure. I made the help put on the fairy lights outside so that there was a festive look about the house. Amrit did the Sikh prayer upstairs and then downstairs in MS's room. Choco also participated enthusiastically in all the festivities but ran to the sanctuary of my arms when crackers and rowdy neighbours scared him.

12.11.15

After feeding MS, I left him in the care of his two sons and sister, as I had a hundred other things to attend to, the most important of which was to get the oxygen cylinders refilled. After a while I stopped for a breather in the balcony that overlooked the park and almost fell off it. In a fit of misplaced kindness, Simar had strapped MS to the wheelchair and had taken him to the park for a breath of fresh air, with Karan and Amrit in tow. They could not even begin to comprehend MS's horror at being paraded thus in the open. People stared at him. If he could, MS would have protested vehemently at such blatant exposure. I called out asking them to bring him back immediately but by then the entire colony knew.

After a while I peeped into MS's room and saw his face tilted abnormally to one side, an eye compressed due to the posture. I cried as I set his face right, I cried into my lunch and finally cried myself to sleep. The evening OPD would be a distraction, and with the luxury of having so many people tending to MS, I decided to go. A change of scene would do me good.

Simar rang up to tell me that I was to meet him and Karan after OPD for coffee. I was pleasantly surprised, for this was a first. Nothing would make me happier than spending quality time with my sons. We first went to the Airtel store to get a plan for the data card, but my head was like a block of wood and nothing would go in. I feared that they would get impatient with me but they were all right. We then went to a place called Tea Leaves and Coffee Beans where I gave in to the temptation of having cold coffee with ice cream. Much later I learnt that I owed this happy hour to Amrit, for she had tutored my sons to be more caring, though their pleasure in my company seemed genuine enough. It took so little to make a mother happy and I wished they would do it more often.

Karan's flight was delayed by fourteen hours. Before leaving, he took his father's pulse, which he found was strong and bounding despite his deteriorating state. This made him think that MS would last for some time longer. Simar went back to work the next morning. That left Amrit and me alone once again. We would take turns to sit by MS. He tried to tell me something but words would not come out of his mouth. He looked pale and no longer smiled that sweet sad smile of his. After the blatant display of his condition in the park, the neighbours came to visit in hordes. When they asked him, 'Doctor Sahib, how are you?' he raised his thumb in a positive gesture and mouthed the word 'fine', though not a sound emerged.

13.11.15

Today is Bhai Dooj. I had come downstairs in the morning to witness a pathetic scene. Amrit sat by her brother's bed with tears coursing down her cheeks; she had put a red tika on his forehead. Looking at his cadaverous form, she exclaimed plaintively, '*Babaji toh ki dua manga? Mere bhra di lambi umr hove* (What blessing should I ask from Babaji? My brother's long life)?' and we both clung to each other and cried.

While at Rakhi the brother pledges protection to his sister as she ties the sacred thread around his wrist, on Bhai Dooj, the sister puts an auspicious tilak on his forehead and prays for his well-being and longevity.

Though MS had stabilised somewhat when the children were here, he began deteriorating rapidly once again. In the midst of this crisis, a woman from the Shakurpur slum area came in labour. She had conceived after years and had been leaking since last night. On examining her I found that the mouth of her uterus was barely open but the baby was passing thick meconium, which meant it was severely distressed and needed an emergency caesarean right away. After my attachment to a tertiary care hospital, I barely took cases at my own nursing home. More importantly, I was in no mental state to take on such a complicated case and wanted to send her to a government hospital but she refused to budge. Thankfully, the labour progressed fast and one of the improbable coincidences shown in Hindi movies came about. In one room my husband's blood pressure was falling steadily from 80/50 to 70/40 and in the labour room a new life was taking birth. Though smeared with meconium, the baby came out crying lustily. Thank God Sunita was still there (she would be leaving for her sister's wedding soon), for she had been handling obstetric cases with me for years. Omana, on the other hand, knew nothing about births and everything about deaths, which would come handy later. The delivery over, I rushed to MS's room and checked the blood pressure myself. It was low but paradoxically his pulse was good, not the thin, thready pulse of a patient in shock. This was puzzling. Quickly, I called for another BP apparatus; to our utter relief the instrument was at fault! MS would survive another day.

That night Amrit asked Sauruv to sleep downstairs to keep an eye on the GDA lest he fall asleep. We suspected that they did double duty elsewhere to earn that much extra. Being sleep-deprived and overworked, they shirked responsibilities whenever they could. Sauruv refused and for the first time Amrit saw him for what he was, though I had repeatedly told her that he was not as nice as he pretended to be in her presence – unctuous, because of the large tip she always gave him. So it came about that during that long, dark, dreadful night, Amrit and I slept downstairs in the room adjacent to MS, along with Choco, who would not stay alone upstairs. The GDA called us in the middle of the night to say that MS was having difficulty in breathing and was waving his hands frantically. His pulse was not as strong as before and his urine output had decreased drastically, which meant that his kidneys had packed up. MS tried to tell me something but could not speak. He held my hand palm upwards and fingers opposed to thumb and made a gesture of putting something in my hand. I will never know what he wanted to tell me, what hidden treasure he wanted to give me that night of all the nights, when he was beyond communication. After he settled somewhat, we went back to the adjoining room and wide awake suffered quietly in our private hells. That night's vigil was the longest, the worst so far.

14.11.15

Amrit had once asked the GDA that, having nursed so many terminally ill patients, how long did he think that MS would last and he made an accurate guess of a week. MS's diet was negligible and I got a drip running. Kamla and Sunita, at their kindly best, made an effort to feed him orally too, though it took time and patience to make him swallow each little sip. I decided to put in a Ryle tube for intragastric feeding. Even as I wrote a prescription and sent the servant to the chemist to buy one, I gave the GDA on duty a bowl of soup to feed MS. When I returned a few minutes later, the soup bowl was empty! How could have MS drunk so much, so fast? Perhaps the GDA had thrown the broth down the drain or worse still down MS's windpipe, which would asphyxiate him. My worst fears were confirmed when MS began having difficulty in breathing. The first oxygen cylinder I opened in desperation leaked. As another cylinder was being pulled from the store, Amrit ran out to tell me that Veera (as she called her brother) was getting cold. I rushed in. His breathing was laboured, his pulse thin, fast and thready, signalling the end. She held his hand and I his feet, as we helplessly watched him die. His eyes rolled up, his extremities darkened, his hands and feet turned cold. What is that indefinable thing which leaves the physical form to convert a human into a body? At 5.29 p.m. he stopped breathing for a minute and took his last breath at 5.30 pm. It was Saturday, the 14th of November 2015. He was sixty-nine years and two months old.

Choco, who had been trained to come down only on a leash with someone, walked downstairs of his own accord exactly at 5.30 p.m., the very moment MS expired. I lifted him to sniff his dead master so that he would not wait up for him night after night. The very Choco who rebelled vociferously at being tied up for his volatile temperament now sat forlorn at the door of his master's room for two days at a stretch without a sound. Not a morsel passed down his throat.

Despite being 'prepared', despite my 'practical medical' perspective, I experienced absolute and utter grief, almost orgasmic in nature, for the first time in my life. People talk about the bravery of cancer survivors. No one talks about those who survive prolonged cancer dying and death. It is a life-changing experience. The ensuing depression, loneliness and ennui suck one into a vortex from which very few emerge unscathed.

Amrit and I, two lost souls in a lonely household, sat on the cold stone steps and sobbed, at a loss what to do next. Omana, who had come but a few days earlier as the angel of death, went about the 'after-death' chores with the indifference of one for whom death was no novelty. Having dealt with the aged and dying in an old people's home, she put cotton in his nostrils lest air go in to bloat his stomach and tied his lower jaw shut with his thata so that the mouth did not remain open when rigor mortis sets in. As his arms lay on his chest, she straightened them and placed them by his side for the same reason.

Soon after, I got a call from the hospital that there were patients waiting for me. I told them in a matter-of-fact manner that my husband had expired and I would not be able to come, as if it was an everyday occurrence. I rang up Simar in Gurgaon. Karan had left a few days back to attend an important GI conference in San Francisco. As it was 4 a.m. there, I left a message on his voice-mail. I also rang up Ruby and told her to inform the rest of my family, while Amrit rang up her side of the family. With the help of my uncle, I tried to donate MS's eyes but learnt that they do not take the cornea of cancer patients. News spread in the neighbourhood. A kindly neighbour arranged for food to be sent, for, according to custom, the stove is not lit in a house with a dead body in it. A cadaveric icebox was brought from the gurdwara, along with mattresses, white sheets and cushions which were arranged in the large hall in the front. Finally, the 'lash room' lived up to its reputation and welcomed another corpse. Of the four bodies that had occupied that spot, MS was the only one whose head was towards the door. Perhaps this would put an end to the macabre purpose of this room, I thought irrationally. To make sure it did not happen again, I had the hall portioned into smaller rooms later so that when my time came my body would lie upstairs in my home.

I sat on the floor, a statue of sorrow, as people came to offer condolences and mouth inanities. Suddenly I got a coughing/choking fit that wouldn't go away. My lungs craved oxygen, but my larynx had gone into spasm and would not let air enter. I had had a similar attack once, for which I needed to be nebulised in the ICU. Today, I was shifted to a bed and a relative's inhaler saved the day. Had it not been for the puffs of budacort, my lifeless form would have joined my husband's in the very room I was so desperate to avoid. We would have gone down in history as the couple who literally could not live without each other – an aged, modern-day version of Romeo and Juliet in the eyes of those who did not know better. Though my breathing improved, despite being the heroine of this tragedy, I was too weak to sit centre stage and Simar took my place.

The funeral was fixed for eleven the next morning, which offended Karan as traditionally the elder son lights the funeral pyre. He had finally rung up at 9.30 p.m., when it was 8 a.m. there. I pacified him, saying that if it was a matter of a few hours, we could have postponed the cremation. Reluctantly, he let us continue with the original plan.

Mona now had to advance her visit, though she had refused to do so earlier to honour her father-in-law's last wish to see his grandson one last time. She arrived with the child and her own mother but did not sit by me or utter a word of comfort. When her mother expressed her condolences, Amrit could not help telling her that it would have done MS a world of good if he had seen Jessy once before he died. She pretended ignorance. 'I did not know he was that bad; otherwise I would have sent them earlier.'

Either it was a blatant lie or Mona had not cared enough to tell her. Moreover, Mona was not a child who needed her mother's consent to come.

At night, I went upstairs to collect the new clothes that MS would wear after a ritual bath for his final journey to the cremation ground. There I found Simar cosily settled in bed with his wife and son, leaving his grieving mother and dead father to fend for themselves downstairs. He was seeing them for the first time after his deputation to Gurgaon, but it's not every day that one's father dies. I lay on the cold floor by the cold body in a cold coffin the whole night and tried to sleep with Amrit and Kamla by my side. The bout of breathlessness had shaken me. Amrit tried to send me upstairs but I said, 'Let me spend the last night with my husband.'

15.11.15

More relatives arrived in the morning, including Mona's father. Ruby had brought some sandwiches, rusk and mathris for breakfast. When I went upstairs to lock up the place before proceeding for the funeral, I found Mona feeding her father quietly in the kitchen. That was all very well, for I could not have played the gracious host just then. What hurt was that not once did she ask me if I had eaten or not.

The final rituals began. The women were shooed out of the room while a very emotional Simar and Paramjit bathed MS's body with raw milk and water. Finally, all spruced up, dressed in new clothes, MS was put on the bier, with shawls from various relatives covering his body. Over this was placed a huge marigold garland. One by one people paid their respects by touching his feet while those close to him cried copiously. After ardaas he was carried by four pallbearers on his final journey to the funeral pyre. Simar lit the fire. With tears streaming down my face, I watched a lifetime go up in flames.

23.11.15

On MS's death, Sauruv had boasted to the nurse that madam was now totally at his mercy and he would take advantage of the situation. He had been doing so even when MS was alive, but barely so. Of the money he took to buy two litres of milk, he'd buy only one and a half litres and spend the rest on his beedi and gutka. As I had suspected all along, Sauruv began to harass me; but I had not expected it would start so soon, with guests still in the house. He had bought three litres of milk last evening and demanded money again today for another three litres. He had opened a ten-kilo bag of wheat five days ago and said it was over today. There was a limit to how much he could be 'allowed' to pilfer, but he would answer me back when I dared question him. Being subservient to an insolent help was beyond me. I was at the end of my tether.

Simar told me to send him packing, but it was not as simple as that. Henceforth, I would be alone in this big old house constantly in need of repair. A lone senior woman would be a soft target for the plumber, electrician and others entering the premises. Strangers could pose as patients and have their way with me. That Sauruv had a family here, that his daughter studied in the government school in the vicinity would deter him from committing a major crime. Keeping a new male house help whom I did not know, during this vulnerable transition phase of my life, was out of the question. Sauruv was a known evil; who knew how the new help would turn out. Moreover, chucking him out could incur his wrath and incite vengeance.

I wanted to let him continue staying free in my outhouse with his family, and utilise his services part-time. I would give him the same amount of money he was getting now but without food. I would lock up the house when I went to work to prevent pilfering. He could work elsewhere during the time I did not need him and earn extra, but he wanted the status quo to continue. Well-wishers advised me to rent out this place and shift to an apartment complex where security was tight and servants were allowed entry only after police verification. However, I took the advice of another who told me not to take any major decisions during the first three months of grieving when it is difficult to think straight. I stayed put.

PART III

MOVING ON

Most mourners left after the final prayer meeting and the funeral feast that was held on the fourth day. I thought people were exaggerating when they said that they were left alone to deal with their grief after the first few days. How could my loved ones desert me when I needed them most, but that is exactly what they did.

Amrit's return ticket was booked for the 30th, fifteen days later. I thought that she would help me tide over the wave of loneliness and loss. But she preponed her tickets and left with her family. So it had been only about her brother all along! The attention and affection she had showered on me during this period was to make sure that I took care of him. To assuage her guilt, she asked Bhabiji to stay in Delhi for a bit longer. This was the first time I needed Bhabiji to stay, and she refused. Ever since I got married, the entire clan would descend from Nainital year after year to escape the harsh winters and stay with us for months. But the one time I needed her she refused! Providence intervened in the form of a property dispute for which she would have to stay back for at least a month.

As for my sons, the less said the better. Karan left for the US in a matter of days and Simar went back to work in Gurgaon. He could have travelled up and down during the initial days but chose not to. Neither offered any form of emotional, social or financial help. Usually, children become protective towards the solitary parent, but not mine. At times, I could not help wondering where I had erred in raising my children. Had I not inculcated in them the right values, given them the best of education, nurtured them with love and care and given them the best I could? Did I not leave a job I loved to start private practice at home so that I could be with them? Wasn't I the one who played with them, helped them with their homework and took them out?

I wondered what made them so uncaring. Perhaps they bore a deep-seated grudge against me for betraying their father with another man. But then, how come they never saw my devotion towards their wronged father when it was their duty to look after him? I also knew that in their heart of hearts they despised him and his miserly ways but only when it concerned them.

Why can't either of them speak a civil word with me? Karan is perpetually irritated and Simar patronising. They either snap at me or talk down to me. It isn't as if I am an illiterate, uncultured woman they are ashamed of. I am the HOD in the gynae department of a corporate hospital and a writer of no mean acclaim. My patients trust me, my neighbours respect me and I have an honourable place in society. How can I not have opinions or desires of my own? Why do they expect me to toe their line?

Karan comes once in a while to empty a quiver of poisonous darts into my heart and goes back, leaving me bleeding and in pain. As Simar once pointed out, 'You two get along max for an hour.'

'Even if we meet after a year,' I wanted to add, but what was the point.

If this is the way he treats me when I am not dependent on him in any way, I shudder to think what my plight will be if I need him financially or otherwise. As for Simar, he wants me to leave everything and live with them in Mumbai. How can he uproot a full-grown tree and transplant it in a new city to be at the mercy of an indifferent daughter-in-law? Till now, it was because of the distance between us that our relationship had remained cordial. Proximity would lead to conflict. How can I give up my independence, the financial security of a regular job, the comfort of living in my own house? Why should I, a professional at the height of my career, give up my job to become a cook and nursemaid in his house for the sake of physical security? I would not even have time to write (caring for a child was a full-time job) and would die of frustration.

As Sister Shivani had said in one of her sermons: 'Your children could have been your enemies in your previous birth and have come to take revenge by tormenting you.' How true! What amazes me more than their attitude is that I tolerate such behaviour. Why? Perhaps on account of a perpetual sense of guilt. Never more. Though scathed and scarred by the hell of Rajan's making, I have survived and moved on. Now that I have nothing to be ashamed of, I have begun practising the axiom 'be careful of what you tolerate, you are teaching people how to treat you' and have profited from it.

For MS's tervi (13th day of death), I went to the Golden Temple with Simar and his family. As I was talking sadly about his father, he cut me short, 'You hated him from the first day of your marriage. In fact, you hated his entire side of the family!' I was shocked beyond measure. He had always been more loving than Karan and expressed it often in the form of hugs and kisses. That he was hiding so much venom within him was beyond contemplation.

'Hate is too strong a word,' I said. 'There is a vast difference between hate and incompatibility. Our incompatibility did not stop me from looking after him to the best of my ability during this period of his life. What gave you the idea that I hated him?'

'You had told me so once long ago.'

'And this is the perfect time to bring it up?' I asked.

'He was just a convenience for you. You do not miss him; you miss what he did in the house and now you will have to do that.'

'And I was not a convenience for him? Did I not care for him and his parents, despite the fact that I "hated" him? Did I not spend my money on him when he shelled out not a penny for his own treatment? Tell me who was more of a convenience and to whom?'

What was the point of telling Simar that despite our flaws we had got used to living with each other; that despite our difference we had never stayed apart in the forty-one years of marriage; that ever since he was diagnosed with cancer, I had forgiven MS his trespasses. Simar did not know how often I hugged his dying father, held his hand and uttered words of consolation. Not even at the worst of times did I think, *marta kyun nahin* (why doesn't he die). Simar would never understand the dynamics of our marriage and I owed him no explanations. That he could say this at a time like this was beyond tolerance.

I broke down and cried my heart out at the Golden Temple, and in these holy precincts, I vowed that come what may never would I be at the mercy of sons who do nothing but rip me to shreds leaving me bleeding and raw. I resolved to live alone and risk a swift death at the hands of an intruder/servant; it was preferable to being hacked slowly to death with a rusty knife by the produce of my womb.

I left the Golden Temple with an overwhelming sense of loss – loss not only of my dead husband but also of my living sons.

I have acquired a new identity now – that of a widow. Will I change my appearance dramatically? No. Will I behave in a manner prescribed for widows? No. The way I deal with my grief is purely a personal matter. Depriving myself of cheer and colour to mourn my husband till the end of my life is not my way of doing it. Of real importance was the devotion with which I looked after him till his last breath and that was all that mattered.

I realised that you do not have to love a person to miss him. Subconsciously, I'd wait for MS to return from his clinic; whenever I heard a car horn that sounded like his, I would tell the servant to go down and get his things. I'd remember his idiosyncrasies and mannerisms and would be filled with longing for my companion of forty-one years who was never to return.

Sad songs would evoke copious bouts of weeping. I would take care to cry alone, for I was horrified to learn that people mocked my grief. They thought that because I had a litany of complaints against MS, my grief was not genuine. They would never understand and I owed them no explanation. Once again, I poured out my grief on paper, writing essays on what it felt like to be alone.

> Not for me the drab colours and other unsavoury aspects of a vidhwa. However, there is one concession I concede to my widowhood – never again will I wear a flower in my hair.

This piece appeared in the *Tribune* and the 'flower in my hair' bit created quite a furore. People known and unknown wrote:

'It is the flower's loss.'

'What fault is it of the flower?'

'We cannot imagine you without your trademark flower.'

Till I was compelled to reply, 'On popular demand, the flower will adorn my tresses again.'

I got phone calls from doctors with whom I was on mere nodding terms to put the flower back in my hair. It was my USP and I appeared incomplete without it. I had once thanked the head of our anaesthesia department for allowing me to wear flowers in the OT under my cap, though I had quickly switched over to artificial ones. Today, he held me by the shoulders, looked pointedly at my flowerless hair and said, 'Madam, what is this?'

Incorrigible flirt that I was, I replied, 'I am waiting to see who will give me the first flower.' The words were out of my mouth and there was no way I could retrieve them.

Coming from a recently bereaved widow, it shocked the daylights out of him. I hope it did not give him the wrong signal, for I had had enough of men to last me a lifetime.

On the whole, it felt good to know that my article evoked such a resounding response. Even my sons urged me to put the flower back where it belonged.

On a cold and foggy Sunday night in December, I was alone for the first time, a month after MS passed on. It was Paramjit's father's death anniversary, so he had taken his mother for their yearly visit to Amritsar. The servant had retired for the night to his quarters. I locked all the doors so that I could feel 'safe' but could not lock out the loneliness. Bogged down by the overwhelming paperwork, visits to various offices and banks, I had begun to sink into depression. Today I also felt physically sick. Pushing away a scarcely touched dinner (there was no one to force me to eat), I lay my head on the dining table overcome by cold sweats and giddiness. I thought it was the end (diabetics are known to have painless heart attacks) and welcomed it. The peace I so craved was not for me, for the survival instinct kicked in and I rang up a cardiologist. Instead of sending an ambulance, the negligent doctor asked me to take another Metolar and sleep.

Though alive, I still felt very unwell the next morning. Nevertheless, I drove to the hospital as I had an OT list. As I was putting my bag in the locker my associate consultant saw me and exclaimed, 'Madam, your face is white as a ghost.'

Quickly she made me lie down and set the requisite machinery moving. Another gynaecologist was called to operate upon my cases while a physician and the cardiologist were summoned for me. Though the ECG was normal, the physician gave me sublingual midazolam and asked me to rest for an hour, after which they would repeat an ECG, but not a moment's rest did I get. The hustle and bustle of the pre-operative room and the cries of a patient in labour wheeled in for an emergency caesarean section would not allow me to close my eyes. Then the nurse came to make me sign various papers and draw blood for an urgent SOB (shortness of breath) profile, which confirms or rules out a cardiac event even before changes appear in the ECG.

I got firsthand knowledge of the functioning of a corporate hospital as a patient and found it sadly wanting. They had drawn blood but not sent the sample to the lab as I had not deposited the money. Why, they could deduct it from my salary later. I was shocked at the way they treated a patient with suspected MI, that too, the head of a department in their own hospital. What if I did not have the requisite amount in my purse? What if something untoward happened while they dilly-dallied? Fuddled with midazolam, I was walking unsteadily towards the locker room for my purse when the doctor in charge came in and admonished me for getting up. My sense of humour intact, I said, 'That SOB won't do my SOB profile till I pay up.'

'What nonsense! You lie down. I'll talk with the GM.'

Meanwhile, Amrit rang up. I told her that I was in the hospital – as a patient, which alarmed her.

'Who is with you?' I was so used to fending for myself that it had not occurred to me to call anybody.

'No one.' At this she rang up everyone. Ruby came with her husband; Simar arrived a while later and completed the admission formalities. I was shifted to a room by afternoon but again rest eluded me. One by one they came – the nurse, the resident doctor, the housekeeping staff, the general duty attendant. They were followed by the dietician, the kitchen staff with the food, the kitchen staff to take away the utensils and doctors from my department to look me up. Only when you are a patient do you realise the disturbance you are subject to as a patient with a 'Do Not Disturb' placard on her door.

Rajan learnt of my admission from Ruby's husband and came visiting. He drank the milk that had come in for me (I dislike milk), ate some of the parathas that had been sent for Ruby from her home as she would be staying with me for the night. The medication made me sleepy, the travelling for the echo to the main branch made me tired and the steady influx of visitors made me cranky. So though Rajan was still there, I fell asleep.

Rajan, I think, was the reason that everyone, including my sons, had backed off. All knew about my attachment to him (though I told Ruby of my detachment from him, she would not believe me for her personal gains) and they thought that he would now be the anchor I needed. Nothing could be farther from the truth.

The disturbance continued unabated the next day. Milky bed tea at 6 a.m., which I could not drink, followed soon after by breakfast. Then the nurse came to take my vitals, housekeeping to clean the room, kitchen staff with soup and sprouts at 11 a.m., doctor's rounds. He ordered discharge as the results were normal. Only when I was back home on my own bed did I get the rest I needed.

Ruby had stayed with me during the stress thallium test and was by my side now during my hospital stay and I was mighty grateful on both accounts, but she too had let me down. During MS's dying days she had made tall promises about visiting me often, staying with me for some time, taking me to movies and outings with them but these remained good intentions. In fact, I had told her that with her second grandchild due, she would not have time for me, but she had retorted emotionally that she could come on weekends when her son was at home to help his wife. She never did and assuaged her conscience by saying, 'Who do I come to when you are always so busy?'

'Why, on the weekends as promised?' I wanted to ask but kept mum.

When she did come, instead of offering solace, Ruby made it a point to say something that made me feel bad about myself for days afterwards. I could do without her toxic remarks. When I suggested going for a movie together, she replied that she had already seen it with her husband. What about her promise about taking me along? Sensing my hurt she added, 'I can see it again with you if you like,' which was not the same thing.

The one thing I really wanted to do was travel, but I had no one to go with. Ruby and MH travelled a lot, so when I delivered her second grandson and she wanted to give me something, I suggested the best gift would be to take me along to whichever place they visited next as I badly needed a change. They went to Mauritius soon after without me. The sooner I realised that people had families of their own to tend to, lives of their own to lead, the better it would be for me.

My brothers would come with their families from abroad and stay with her. This was because she was a housewife and I a working woman. Moreover, her husband would entertain them lavishly and shower gifts. As there was no way I could match their extravagance, I felt small, unwanted and unloved, alienated and alone in the dark, outside their golden circle. This diminished my sense of self-worth to such a degree that I shrivelled up. Instead of realising that I was on the verge of clinical depression and needed their support, they discussed me unfavourably behind my back and Ruby made it a point to pour all that negativity into my ears once they left, reducing me to an emotional mess. This only served to reinforce the buttressing of the citadel I had begun to build around my vulnerability.

Gradually, I began setting my house in order. Of prime importance was the installation of CCTV cameras. They were an expensive but wise investment. Surprisingly, my own employees were up in arms against it. I thought I was protecting myself from outside elements; they saw it as something that would curb their nefarious activities. Sauruv would no longer be able to take large quantities of rations and cook food for his family. Sapna, I learnt later, was given to smoking, drinking and soliciting customers. Sunita had not yet returned from her sister's wedding and I thought that Sapna was brave to live downstairs alone, little suspecting that she preferred having a free run of the place. The day the cameras were installed, she left – good riddance.

MS had made such a fuss about his cupboard and mine and now he had left it all behind for me to do as I wished. His watches, including the quaint breast pocket silver one with a chain, I gave to Simar, for he was a collector of watches. As for money, except for a few bundles of crisp new ten- and twenty-rupees notes, there was hardly any. For every cupboard I emptied with Sauruv's help, I had to give him something – a jacket, a T-shirt, a backpack – and listen to him complain about the extra work. The ones Sauruv rejected I gave to the sweeper, street vendors, guards, labour working at a nearby construction site. Those left over, I stuffed in bags and sent to an old people's home. I kept a tied turban and a pair of his specs for remembrance. Some of his woollens I wore. They gave me the snug warmth I never got from him.

Little did I think that pornography would make me cry but the collection I came upon hidden in his almirah told a sorry tale. The explicit pictures looked accusingly at a wife who had denied their owner his conjugal rights, forcing him to seek release in this manner. That his sexual inadequacies were one of the reasons his wife had strayed was another matter. A few days later, a cousin from abroad came over to offer condolence.

'You know what I was getting for you?' she asked.

'What?'

'A vibrator.'

'I wouldn't be caught dead with it, though alive, I could have ...' I said.

'What do you mean?'

'I would have liked to experience the pleasure it offered a woman but am mortified at the thought of my children finding it after my death!'

Setting the house in order was one thing, but managing MS's affairs outside was another matter. First and foremost, I had to collect his death certificate from the MCD office. After much red tape I held the document in my hand and thought, 'An entire human being reduced to a piece of paper,' and put my husband or what remained of him in my pocket – something I had never been able to do during his lifetime.

That MS had not left a registered will behind led to many avoidable issues at the bank, post office, etc. Though I had got MS to make one on plain paper, it was not accepted at all places. As I was complaining about this to Simar, instead of commiserating with me, he asked me bluntly, 'Have you made yours?' which shocked me into registering my will within a week.

I had to make multiple visits to various banks near MS's clinic, which was twelve kilometres away. Much to my embarrassment, the bank officer was surprised that I did not know whether my husband had a locker or not, but that was MS for you. A number of such lockers remain sealed and crores of rupees lie unclaimed in banks because people don't register their wills. I do concede that when people showed their cards to their heirs before their death, they have been cheated and thrown out of their very own homes. But when the cancer resurfaced, MS was one of the few who knew that time was running out and could have set his papers in order. It would have saved me the effort of running alone from pillar to post. Once again, I wondered at the gesture he made holding my hand palm upwards to put something in it and what he was trying to tell me when it was too late and he could no longer speak.

I asked the bank officer to go through MS's bank statement as the bank deducts the locker rent directly from the account. Thus I came to know that he did have a locker and even got the locker number. All I had to do was find the key, which was easier said than done. If I could not produce it, the lock would be broken in front of authorised officials after a lot of red-tapism. Even in death, MS continued to annoy me. To cut a long story short, I eventually got the key and found a mere lakh in the locker, but it was hard-earned money, considering the effort I went through to acquire it.

Then there was the question of the nursing home downstairs, which I could not run because MS had not transferred the property in my name. The mutation took almost a year. I was charged an exorbitant fee for this, of which I knew that the middleman appropriated a hefty sum, but there was nothing I could do about it. Despite closing down the nursing home, I was being charged commercial rates for electricity and water. During that period my monthly expenditure was eighty thousand rupees on an average and I was at my wits' end. So to the electricity and water departments I trudged alone with evidence regarding the closure of the commercial enterprise. After months of endeavour this problem too was sorted out and my utility bills came down to domestic levels.

MS had left so little for me because he had invested all in acquiring his clinic. Better the shop than any bank balance he would have left behind, for its value had increased. However, there was a hitch in this inheritance too. The court needed a 'no-objection certificate' from both my sons. Willingly, they obliged. What I did with the shop, which was quite a distance away from my home, was my business now. Leaving it untended would invite illegal occupants. The moot point was whether to sell it or rent it out. I did not want to sell a place that had been dearer to MS than life itself. Rajan too was of the same opinion, though for a different reason. Property rates were rising, while money would devalue over time, so we began to look for a tenant. Renting it out to a doctor would be ideal for both parties as the doctor would get a readymade practice, a furnished clinic and a stock of medicines, but we were unable to find one. Finally, we got a Muslim tenant, who would run a hair salon there. MS would be turning in his grave at the idea of a barber in his shop, but I had to do with what I got.

Rajan took me to the court to get a rent agreement signed with the tenant. The old Rajan would have held me close and consoled me or at least have held my hand while driving, but this one was aloof. All the way he talked on the phone about huge business deals, which impressed me not a bit. Not a word of comfort, not a gesture of reassurance came from him when my life was at its lowest ebb. On the contrary, he was condescending, rubbing in the fact that he had to miss an important appointment on my account. I hated myself for still needing him for property matters, but there was no one else I could turn to.

Then there was the question of clearing up the clinic, which was cramped with new almirahs, new settees, a fridge and medicines that MS bought in wholesale. I wanted Rajan around to deal with the various technicians, who would dismantle the aluminium partition, take down the AC and TV, etc. I needed him to arrange for the truck, supervise its loading and unloading at my place. Except for replacing his impatient look with a bored, martyred one, he did nothing to help while I toiled on for hours. The only time he was galvanised into action was when, without asking me, he told his driver, 'You wanted a TV? Here take this.' I could only look on helplessly and consider it payment for his reluctant help. I ordered food for all of us. While the old Rajan would have insisted on paying, he looked on as I settled the bill. It was late night by the time the clinic that MS had so lovingly set up was dismantled and the truck unloaded at my house. I couldn't have possibly let a horde of strange men have a free run of my place without a man around. So despite myself, I begged Rajan to accompany me home. He left after dinner without a single word or gesture of affection.

After that, whenever I needed him for anything he would promise to come and stand me up at the last moment. On each of the three occasions he pretended that an emergency had cropped up. When I finally got the message, I looked at MS's photo hanging on the wall and had the longest conversation I ever had with him.

'Strange as it may seem to you, what you could not achieve in life, you have managed to do in death. No matter in how many ways Rajan had wronged me over the years, I never thought that there would come a day when I would tell him that MS was better than you. At least you said no at the very outset and gave no illusion of hope, whereas he promises to come and does not turn up. You must be having the last laugh from somewhere up there.

'All the time I was with Rajan,' I continued my monologue, 'he would tell me to leave you and go with him, so I presumed that with you out of the way he would come galloping like a knight in shining armour. We would do all the things we had wanted to do together without shame or guilt, but of course he couldn't care less. Perhaps harming you, not loving me, had been his sole intention ever since you had set goons after him to retrieve your wife. I wish you were alive to see this complete break from that bastard. Though you hurt me in a hundred different ways, you were right about him all along. I thank you from the bottom of my heart for not setting me free when I wanted to link my fate with his.'

I finally began receiving a tidy rent from the clinic, which eased my financial woes somewhat. Ironically, MS served me better in death than alive. Never in his lifetime did he give me the warmth that his jackets gave me in the first winter of my widowhood. Never did he give me money he earned from this very clinic, from which I now received a monthly sum. Never did he share with me the secrets that tumbled out of his cupboards. He was more of a husband I wanted now, than he was ever in his lifetime.

I have much to be grateful for. That he was never kind and caring helped me move on faster, for I had nothing to miss. A hot water bottle to warm my feet and pillow to hug had served my purpose then and would serve my purpose now; Choco was my companion then as he was now. That MS never took care of me during illness had prepared me to fend for myself. That he did not accompany me on night calls, as husbands of doctors who cared for their wives did, has made me strong. Once I overcame the fear of living alone, and learnt to perform the chores of a householder that fell on his shoulders, I was ready to be on my own.

Given the choice, I would any day have preferred a kind, loving and generous husband who I'd miss terribly now.

In the third week of December, I would be leaving for Mumbai to babysit Jessy, as his maternal grandparents would be gone for a while. The change would do me good. As I was packing, Rajan turned up to apologise and wish me goodbye. I forgave him as usual. We actually spoke this time and I told him that while my punishment for our indiscretion was over with MS's death, he still bore the cross of his paralysed wife. Without meaning to, I triggered a monologue on the amount she was costing him. I told him that whatever improvement had to occur after a stroke occurred within a year. He could cut down the expense of three nurses round the clock and keep a full-time maid instead. He did not answer. Perhaps, they were taking care of his 'needs' too and his wife was just a pretext to keep them in the house.

He promised that he would pick me up from the airport when I returned and all was right with my world again. It would be good to feel safe and loved again. Despite having a son and sister in the NCR, I had to depend on Rajan's assistance and I accepted it gratefully. I was too scared to travel alone in a taxi from the airport at night. I would be returning to an empty life in an empty home on a foggy December night and looked forward to his company in the cosy confines of the car. Why did I always believe in him when he had repeatedly proved untrustworthy? True to form, he rang me up when I was in Mumbai to say that he would not be able to come as an urgent 'money matter' had cropped up and he would send his driver instead. A person who owed him a large sum of money had expired and his sons refused to acknowledge the debt as he had no proof. He would be going to Chandigarh to attend the funeral and sort out the matter.

'A funeral is not the right time to talk of such matters with bereaved sons.' I spoke to a dead phone.

As I sat in his car with a heavy heart, I asked the driver who had died in Chandigarh. To my utter surprise he replied, 'No one.'

'Then why has your master gone there?'

'He has taken his wife with a nurse to a miracle healer someone has strongly vouched for.'

It was as if he had thrust a dagger in my breast. Nothing Rajan said or did again could redeem this breach of trust. The 'patni-vrata' bastard could have done it on any other day but this. As for the nurse he took along, I am sure he had ulterior motives. It was as if I was widowed twice over.

I had never felt so bereft, forsaken, not even after I had given up on Simar at Amritsar within two weeks of MS's death. The intensity of my pain amazed me. It threatened to devour me alive. Just then a random message on WhatsApp redeemed my sense of self-worth. It read: 'God sometimes takes people from your life to protect you. Don't run after them.'

Rajan was certainly not worth running after; he never had been. He was just a thorn embedded in my flesh for so long that I had got used to the pain. It was time I pulled it out. The jolt of abandonment(s) shook me of my dependency on others. Rajan was the last bastion to fall. In retrospect, I realised that it was the best thing that could have happened to me. I set about rebuilding my life – alone.

Yoga was one of the best ways to heal my battered mind, body and soul. During summers I luxuriated in stretching my limbs underwater and let a sense of well-being wash over me. The pleasurable fatigue of a difficult operation performed well, the joy of saving a life, the miracle of birth that never ceased to amaze despite witnessing it so often as an obstetrician, all gave me a satisfaction granted to a fortunate few. I was happy reading a good book and happier still writing one. Emotions bubbled in my mind like subterranean springs to explode into words that to my happy surprise got published.

Eleven months later, when I invited people for my husband's vareena, the standard exclamation was '*Saal ho gaya? Pata bhi nahin chala* (It's been a year? We didn't even realise).' Indeed! *Unko kyun pata chalega. Ek ek din ka toh mujhe pata chala hai* (Why would they realise; I was the one who knew how each day passed).

Independence was a hard-earned ally that stands me in good stead. The yawning void of companionless Sundays, the crying to sleep on a lonely bed, the bruises on my soul, the blister on my heart, all were secret wounds that I hid from the world under a cheerful facade as I stumbled towards self-sufficiency. I was like a bull whose mate falls dead under the yoke and he has to till the field of life alone. It has two choices – either buckle under the weight or pull along, come what may. I chose to do the latter.

The first time I ventured for a movie alone I looked around the hall surreptitiously as if I had come to meet a secret lover; even the feeling of guilt was similar. Out of embarrassment, I did not come out of the hall during the interval, though I would have loved to buy a bucket of popcorn. However, by the end, I figuratively patted myself for doing it, and why not? If I could shoulder the drudgery single-handedly, why not the joys of life? After all, one does not die with the dead. Life goes on and you choose how you live it – with a cascade of laments against those who forsook you, the departed, or by enjoying your blessings. I chose the latter and have emerged all the more capable and confident.

Acknowledgements

My heartfelt gratitude to

Jhumri, my adorable Shih Tzu, for her quiet companionship during the solitary business of writing.

Jashn, Aanya and Alia for the distraction and cheer they bring to brighten my Sundays.

The brave-hearts I encountered during my career as a doctor who valiantly fought cancer, and their caregivers, unsung heroes who stood by them through victory or defeat.

Nitin Valecha for seeing that thing in my manuscript worthy of Bloomsbury.

Jaishree with her happy voice and sound editing, who with surgical precision cut off the dead portions, even as she uttered kind and soothing words.

Last but not the least I cannot even begin to thank Krishan Chopra for the effort he put in, for the numerous discussions we had over luncheons, for painstakingly going over the manuscript over and over again and pruning it ruthlessly to bring it to its present crisp state.

About the Author

Dr Amrinder Bajaj is a gynaecologist with over four decades of experience. Previously HOD of Obstetrics and Gynaecology at MAX Multi Specialty Centre, Pitampura, she is now attached with the Fortis Memorial Research Institute, Gurugram.

Among the books that she has published is a memoir based on her association with Khushwant Singh, two wellness books and an autobiographical novel. She writes on and off for the *Times of India, Tribune* and *Indian Express*.